FIFE'S
TRAMS AND BUSES

A W BROTCHIE

Published by N B Traction, 31 Forfar Road, Dundee

£7.95

First Published 1990

© A W Brotchie

ISBN 0 905069 27 7

3. *This book would be less complete without the contribution of the late Matthew Cousin. He drove buses – firstly with his brothers in 1909 , then for SGO Co. and Alexanders until retiral aged 76 (then the oldest PSV driver with the Scottish Transport Group). His encyclopaedic memory and collection of photographs enriched this work. He is pictured here (left) at Charlestown in 1960.*

Cover Views:
1. *To replace the Kirkcaldy trams, Alexander supplied a fleet of Albions of this type. These were the first vehicles to operate in Kirkcaldy with the Alexander fleet name. This one, photographed at the foot of Whytescauseway, was 196, MS 8289.*
2. *Dunfermline operated its trams for six years after Kirkcaldy had abandoned theirs. Car 22 was photographed at Cowdenbeath depot.*

Typeset by Trinity Typesetting, Edinburgh. 031-553 6902.
Printed and bound by Spectrum Printing Company, Livingston

INTRODUCTION

THIS history of the development of road passenger transport in the Kingdom of Fife has proved to be a labour of love which has occupied over twenty years' research – albeit not continuous. While many facts have been extracted from dusty files of old newspapers, licensing records and Council minutes, the flesh of the story has been added to these bare bones by the invaluable reminiscences of many former employees of the pioneering companies. Some of these men and women have passed away since time of interview and their memories are recorded only here.

It is extremely likely that there are gaps in the story – perhaps some fleeting enterprises have passed unrecorded. For that I can only apologise. A bus operator did not have to apply to Parliament, or even (for some time) his local Council before setting up in business, and contemporary records of the motor bus industry in Fife are minimal. Original documentation is almost non-existent for most bus operators. An advertisement, a time-table or a ticket may be the only tangible record.

Tramway operators were tied by legislation and their proposals and statistics were recorded by the Board of Trade as forerunner of the Department of Transport.

This history is presented in two sections – firstly, a geographically oriented history of the development of the passenger transport industry, dealt with in areas which roughly equate to today's District divisions of Fife. In the second part, a detailed description of each of the many and varied operators of both buses and tramcars is presented.

An attempt has been made to list information for each business in the same manner so that comparisons may, if required, be drawn. For bus operators no attempt has been made to chart the individual history of each vehicle once it fell into the grasp of the 'combine'. For that information readers are directed to the invaluable reference fleet lists produced by the Omnibus Society/PSV Circle, to which acknowledgment is gratefully recorded. Information on the vehicles is generally such as is not available elsewhere but again one can only be conscious of the enormous gaps and the number of question-marks which have to appear. Despite a through search of Motor Tax records in the days when they were still kept in Cupar there are many blanks. Even then the records were scanty with virtually no details of vehicles in the period before June 1921.

Vehicle information is listed in columns: (1) fleet number if applicable; (2) date of acquisition or registration; (3) registration number; (4) engine/chassis manufacturer; (5) manufacturer's reference number; (6) builder of bodywork; (7) type and seating of body using conventional format, ie. Prefix letter for type of body, Ch charabanc, Ly lorry, Ly/ch interchangeable body, B bus, C coach, L low bridge, followed by seating capacity, followed by suffix letter for door position, F front, R rear, D dual; (8) any other relevant information, – ni nothing further known.

Very many people have worked over the years on Fife's trams and buses – some for short times as holiday relief conductors – some for a lifetime. It has not been possible to speak to each and every individual but of the very many I have spoken to, nobody, without exception, has been other than helpful and obliging. If anybody can add an old photograph or a reminiscence or correction I would be most grateful if they would contact me – any such information will be incorporated into a revised second edition.

A W Brotchie
Aberdour, Fife.

April 1990

4. *Dunfermline's High Street in 1925, photographed from the top deck of a tram which is waiting (patiently?) for the approaching bus to pass. The street was then the main road from Dunfermline to the west, prior to construction of the Glen Bridge. Tilling-Stevens bus (SGO Co MS 2967) is completing its journey from Stirling.*

FIFE'S TRAMS AND BUSES

The 'Kingdom of Fife' can perhaps be best described geographically as the large land mass filling the gap in Scotland's eastern coastline between the Firths of Forth and Tay. Its position, those two major obstacles north and south, and the west-east flowing rivers Leven and Eden all combined to frustrate the early traveller heading northwards from Edinburgh. The lowest bridgings of the Forth and Tay were, until the twentieth century, as far upstream as Stirling and Perth respectively, all other traffic having perforce to submit to various ferry crossings, often hazardous and frequently unreliable.

Proud of its identity, the county successfully resisted the 1975 reorganisations to be split administratively, with the northern half merging into Tayside and the balance absorbed by Lothian. The character of the 512 square miles of the Kingdom varies greatly, from the rich agricultural lands of Stratheden to the industrial areas which found their wealth in coal. Of about 300,000 wage earners in 1920, no less than half were then employed in mining. This dependence has racially changed over the years with new high technology industries creating a new major source of employment, and the winning of coal, other than by open cast methods, is confined to the Longannet complex.

Cupar, the County town, lies rather isolated in the North-East, the main population centres being Dunfermline (population in 1921 47,000), and Kirkcaldy (49,000 at that date). Coastal settlements varied from coal exporting harbours to the busy fishing ports of the East Neuk – Anstruther, Pittenweem and Crail. St Andrews, historic defensive site, home of University and golf, commands the North-East corner.

Until the end of the eighteenth century travel in and across the Kingdom would generally be by horse, with but few merchants' carts attempting the unmetalled tracks. Improvements to these roads were instigated under the Turnpike Roads Acts (where a toll was extracted for the use of a higher standard of 'carriageway'). This covered the 'Great North Road' – Edinburgh to Inverness via Queensferry and Perth – from 1753. Post coaches followed this route but did not always make provision for passengers. The first recorded *stage*-coach i.e. one which operated a regular passenger oriented service, is said to have commenced in 1805 between the ferry ports of Pettycur (near Kinghorn) and Newport, by way of Kennoway. Others followed, linking the Forth and Tay ferries by differing routes. Services on the Great North Road also increased and in the early 1830s the *Dunfermline Register* recorded the 'Defiance', 'Wonder', 'Waterloo', 'No Wonder', 'Antiquary', 'Royal William', 'Aurora' and 'Coburg' – all evocative of the period. From Pettycur at one time or another ran the 'Aberdeen', 'Royal Union', 'Montrose Highlander', 'Kingdom of Fife' and 'Tally Ho'. The 'Defiance' of Messrs Ramsay and Barclay was held to be the pick of the crop but even so, it was said that a journey from Edinburgh to Dundee across Fife was a 'serious business for a thinking person' – echoing the heartfelt cry of the old Edinburgh worthy, 'Fareweel Scotland, I'm awa' tae Fife'.

5. *The posting establishment in Crail ran daily coaches from Crail to Anstruther, and Crail to St. Andrews. This early scene was photographed in 1883 at the entrance to Cambo Estate, Kingsbarns – between Crail and St. Andrews. Horses were purchased from the Edinburgh Street Tramways Company. They no doubt preferred the East Neuk breezes to Auld Reekie's pollution!*

6. *Cousins' Culross horse bus outside the City Arms Hotel in Bridge Street, Dunfermline in the early 1900's. (This is now the City Hotel).*

7. *St. Catherine's Wynd, Dunfermline was the starting point for the Kelty bus run by Robert Philip. 'No 13' was licensed to seat 18 and has the side sheets down to offer some protection on this winter's day. With eighteen folk within, the atmosphere could perhaps be described as 'cosy'!*

8. *Possibly the last horse bus in Fife was that which ran from Falkland to Falkland Road Station. The well turned out carriage was photographed prior to World War I. After the war there was much support for a light railway to cover the 2.75 miles.*

Stage coaches held only a short dominance in distance travel across Fife — within twenty years the coming of railways had virtually seen their eclipse. Fife's first passenger railway, the Edinburgh and Northern, eventually joined the ferry ports of Burntisland and Newport (which became the bases for train-ferries also) from 1850. With the opening of the East Fife railway it was recorded that Fife's last stage coach, the 'Balcarres', ran on its final journey in August 1854 between Kirkcaldy and Anstruther. This was not in fact the case, as the yellow-painted 'Loch Leven Castle', run by the tyrannical Mrs Stocks of Kirklands Hotel, Kinross, was still plying its regular route from Milnathort to Burntisland. Latterly cut back to run only to Cowdenbeath (fare inside 2/-, outside 1/6d) it made its final trip on 1 September 1860, the coach and horses festooned with wreaths and flowers and the hotel flag at half-mast. Thus ended Fife's stage coach days.

As railways advanced through the Kingdom various bus or coach feeder services came and went, some lasting only a few months operating from a temporary railhead, some lasting many years longer. Perhaps the longest lasting was that linking Falkland Road Station with Falkland village. Although a light railway was surveyed, and authorised, to replace the bus and also serve the distillery at Newton of Falkland, the plans were abandoned after the First World War, by which time the horse-bus had also ceased.

Regular horse-bus services had operated on other routes, one between Crail and St Andrews dating from before 1845 and maintained until the railway connection was completed in 1883.

In the west of the county, around Dunfermline, a comprehensive selection of horse-bus services was available, serving the surrounding villages. The earliest records, from 1890, list regular, if not frequent, operations to Culross and Torryburn (Messrs Blackwood and Herdman), Limekilns (Elder and Clarke), Kelty (Rintoul), Saline (Crombie and Kerr) and Lochgelly (Robert Philp). In 1897 services were added to Lassodie (McEwan) and Townhill (Simpson). Rintoul gave up his business, which was then taken over by Sheriff and in 1900 Templeman took over Crombie's runs on the Saline route, which had been run for a short time by a Mr McGibbon.

In 1901 Tom Cousins took up operations on the Culross run, starting an association which was to last for a quarter of a century. An Inverkeithing run was started by James Wilson of Hospitalhill in 1902. Dunfermline magistrates granted licences to the various operators and vehicles, in August 1902 registering twelve owners with 26 brakes and 14 wagonettes between them.

The changing pattern is recorded over the early years of the new century; John Todd took over the Townhill run, James Beattie that to Kelty; then in 1903 William Philp of St Margaret Street, Dunfermline took over Keir's Saline service. Other operators came and went — Todd stopped his Townhill run but restarted when he thought conditions warranted.

Kirkcaldy has no similar record of country horse bus routes. By the late nineteenth century buses ran the length of the 'Lang Toun'; Messrs Miller and Kay ran alternately between Gallatown and Newtown. Scully's bus ran from Newtown to Dysart.

9. *The Dunfermline to Saline horse bus run by William Philp became such a local institution that it featured in picture postcards! The licence for this vehicle was granted in January 1903 — to seat 12 inside and 4 outside.*

10. *Postcard view of the 'Limekilns Bus', a three-horse brake, well laden with a brass band en route to a regatta — but which band and which regatta?*

Fife was crossed in both directions by rail by the end of the nineteenth century. North to South travel was greatly facilitated by the official opening of the (first) Tay Bridge on 1 June 1878, and its more permanent replacement on 13 July 1887, followed by the construction of the magnificently engineered cantilever bridge across the Forth, opened on 4 March 1890; but railways did not always satisfy the requirements of urban and inter-urban movement. Horse tramways had replaced horse buses in many cities, the much lessened resistance of iron wheels on rails instead of on unmetalled roads giving a much more efficient use of available horse power. A variety of mechanical inventions was utilised to replace or augment horse-flesh, and on Dundee's hills, for example, small steam locomotives were used to haul large tramcars. A similar scheme was, in 1883, authorised to serve the length of Kirkcaldy but canny Fifers were reluctant to invest, consequently it did not come to fruition. Tramways were further popularised by the successful application of electricity as motive force and in the earliest years of this century many and varied schemes were proposed within the County.

Fife's first electric tramway was conceived by Kirkcaldy Town Council who obtained Parliamentary Authority for several lines in the town. The first of these, from Gallatown (where a substantial red sandstone depot was built) by way of the Path and High Street to West End of Linktown opened on 28 February 1903. Ten cars were purchased and such was its success that construction of what became known as the 'Upper Route' from Junction Road by the Railway Station to Whytescauseway soon followed. This, including a short branch to Beveridge Park gates, opened on 28 September 1903. A further twelve cars were obtained. Kirkcaldy's tramways served an expanding town but the original – 'Lower' – route suffered by having been built as single track with infrequent passing places where the tram had to wait to meet that travelling in the opposite direction. This slowed up journeys, and the mistake was not repeated on the Upper route which was constructed generally as double line.

11. *Tram number 7 in Kirkcaldy High Street during the first few days of operation. The old Town House is on the right. This area is now pedestrianised.*

12. *Whytescauseway, terminus for 'Upper Route' cars to Junction Road and for through cars to Leven. Car 9 of the first batch, photographed c 1905.*

13. *Gallatown car sheds – the building was used by Alexander's buses after the trams were abandoned, then by T Muir, but has been recently demolished.*

14. *Car 16 leaving Dysart terminus, heading for Junction Road. photographed c. 1913.*

15. *Cars of the Corporation fleet in Gallatown Depot c 1910. The differences between the first batch of cars (7 and 6 on the left) and the second batch (on the right) are most evident when the stairs to the upper deck are compared.*

16. *A highly sought-after position, working on the new electric trams, is reflected in the pride in their appearance. Crews often worked together for years; Kirkcaldy Driver J Gillies and Conductor A Balfour.*

The benefits of tramways over the slow horse-bus alternative were not difficult to perceive and soon plans were prepared by R G E Wemyss, Laird of the estates lying to the east of Kirkcaldy, for an ambitious 8-mile tramway across his lands, linking the coastal mining villages to Kirkcaldy in the west and Leven to the east. While greatly aiding movement of workers, this scheme had the added utility of diverting traffic away from the old coastal road through Buckhaven and Methil, an area which was subsequently used for (his) colliery expansion.

The tramway was constructed by Mr Wemyss and only when complete was it handed over to an operating company. Regular operation began on 25 August 1906 from Leven as far as Kirkcaldy's Gallatown terminus, then after negotiation and agreement, from 27 September cars ran through by the "Upper Route" to Whytescauseway in the centre of the town. This gave passengers on the Wemyss trams a connection to Kirkcaldy station and improved longer distance travel from the coastal towns. The only prior route had been to change, and wait, at Thornton Junction from the main line for the infrequent Buckhaven branch train. To run on the new tram-

17. *Wemyss car 2 photographed in 1906. The scene is at the top of White Swan Brae, with the hotel under construction on the left – below, on the right, the bustling coal-filled rail sidings serving Methil Docks, exporting from the local mines.*

18. *Four of these large bogie cars (numbers 14 - 17) were bought by the Wemyss Coal Company for transporting miners, but they soon passed to the Tramway Company where their large carrying capacity was much appreciated. Photographed at Leven terminus.*

way nine small single deck cars were purchased – top seated cars being prohibited because of the 'light railway' nature of the line. Four similar cars were soon added to accommodate unanticipated demand and the Wemyss Coal Company purchased four long bogie trams for use by miners going on and coming off shift. These were soon added to the Company fleet to create a total fleet of seventeen cars which sufficed for most of the line's existence. When through running between Leven and Whytecauseway was in operation (it ceased during World War I) one Corporation car was used to every three Company cars – but no top deck passengers were permitted on the Kirkcaldy vehicles.

A mini tramway-mania gripped Fife when the success of the Wemyss line became apparent and three further schemes were surveyed. The first centred on Dunfermline, linking with Lochgelly via Cowdenbeath, plus branch lines to Inverkeithing, Rumblingwell and Townhill. The second was for a long coastal line from Inverkeithing to Kirkcaldy by way of Aberdour and Burntisland; the third linked Kirkcaldy, Thornton and Auchterderran to Lochgelly with branches serving Cardenden and Lochore.

19. *Opening day scene on the Wemyss tramway, at East Wemyss, with large numbers of local children showing their interest.*

20. *Another early scene, at Shorehead, Leven. One of the bare-footed lads is apparently retrieving a coin or a pin from the rails after the car had flattened it. Pins became 'Swordies'!*

21. *Leven Shorehead by John Patrick of Leven, who took several fine record photos of the early days of the tramways.*

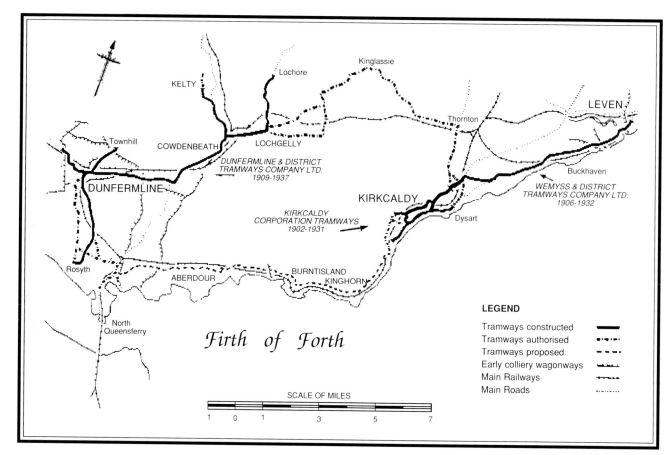

22. *Map showing Fife's tramways, both proposed and constructed.*

23. *Dunfermline Tramways car 16 leaving the town's East Port Street on the start of its journey to Lochgelly. The track here was doubled, in 1921.*

24. *Car 11 in Chalmers Street, after opening of the Rumblingwell route. On the left is Pittencrieff Street, opposite where the Glen Bridge was built in 1932, the buildings on the right demolished, including Masterton's furniture shop.*

Of these only the first became more than a proposal and Parliamentary Authority lay dormant until acquired by the Balfour Beatty organisation. They had just completed at Townhill, north of Dunfermline, a large electricity generating station for their subsidiary Fife Electric Power Company. The new owners lost little time in building the tramway, the first section opening between Dunfermline and Cowdenbeath on 2 November 1909. Extensions took the trams of the Dunfermline and District Tramways Company to Lochgelly, to Kelty, to Lochore (after transferring powers granted to another developer), to Rumblingwell and finally to Rosyth. The planned line to Inverkeithing was never built although a small amount of preparatory work was done. Eventually the Company operated forty-five tramcars, most being similar open-topped vehicles. The common gauge of Fife's tramways was 3ft 6ins, so had all the proposed lines been built, an inter-connecting network of over sixty miles would have served most of the larger settlements of the southern half of the County. Other tramways suggested included a line from Dunfermline to Culross via Torryburn and a link from Crossgates to Aberdour. The heyday of Fife's tramways came *before* World War I; afterwards the motor bus

26. *Lochgelly Road, Lumphinnans, looking east towards Lochgelly, photographed in 1909, just after the cars started running. Has the whole population appeared for the photographer?*

27. *Bank Street, Lochgelly, with tram 19. This was the terminus before the Lochore extension opened. Shawls are the required dress for the girls on the left.*

28. *Car 3 at Kelty terminus in 1913 with the terminus conveniently between the two 'Goths'. The man on the left, risking his life by standing in the middle of the road, already sports an artificial leg – probably from a pit accident.*

25. *The rural nature of much of the Dunfermline tramway is evident in this typical scene. Single track with loops for passing delayed journeys and much track was doubled in the 1920's. Car 27 heading towards the start of Dunfermline's ribbon development.*

29. *The deserted terminus at Townhill. The driver of car 24 may be expecting poor weather – he has his waterproofs folded over the stair handrail.*

was more technically reliable and could be obtained on hire-purchase by any entrepreneur; also, the release of many War Department chassis in the immediate post-war period boosted this infant industry.

It is necessary to turn the clock back, to the years before the Great War, to uncover the earliest motor bus services in Fife. Contrary to previously expressed statements the honours appear to go, not to Tom Cousins of Culross, but to the grandiosely entitled West Fife Motor Traction Company Ltd, who started a service between Cowdenbeath (Fountain) and Kelty on 5 February 1909. After tramway proposals had been fruitlessly discussed for years a Kirkcaldy architect, J D Swanston, registered this Company on 1 February 1909. Capital was 2,500 shares of £1, the six directors undertaking to take 50 each. These other directors were a cross section of Fife respectability – three doctors (from Cowdenbeath, Lochgelly and Cardenden), two chemists and a master printer were signatories to the incorporation. The stated object was to operate motor buses from Cowdenbeath to Cardenden, Lochore and Kelty, also to Aberdour during the summer months, using vehicles 'as approved for use in London'. On 4 February the first trial trip was made, the decorated bus taking Cowdenbeath dignatories to Crossgates. Speeches heralded the new era in local transport – 'the tramways will be superfluous'. The vehicle was a 25-30 HP Arrol-Johnston, and all seemed set for a prosperous future. The Company Secretary, D Hetherington, advertised an ambitious time-table listing (daily) eleven trips to Lochgelly, one to Glencraig, one to Bowhill, one to Crossgates and four to Kelty; – all this with just the one vehicle, although two more were said to be on order. The enterprise had an extremely short tenure as it was stated that the capital required was not forthcoming (surprising as in this short time 1465 share applications were received); the last run was on 4 March, the vehicle (which had been on hire) being returned to its supplier. The pioneer venture had lasted a mere 28 days. The Company was wound up in July. ·

Perhaps the local horse-bus operators had observed the experiment with interest as, at the Dunfermline Magistrates' meeting on 23 June 1909, motor buses were licensed to both George Scott of Culross (a 15-seat Arrol-Johnston) and to Thomas Cousins, also of Culross (two vehicles, a 10-seat Albion and a 15-seat Halley). Scott ran to Culross and Torryburn four times daily, Cousins to Culross thrice daily. Both used Dunfermline's Chalmers' Street as their stance. At this time the other stances were East Port Street for Kingseat and Kelty, Townhill, Lassodie and Lochgelly; Wilson's Inverkeithing bus ran from the foot of New Row, and Harley, the operator to Charlestown and Limekilns, used Abbey Gates. George Scott's daughter, Mrs Jessie Sneddon, thought that her father's first bus was purchased in 1907, but that even then it was not the first in the area. The contemporary local press reports of the West Fife Company's enterprise are couched in such a manner as to suggest that **it** was the first. Perhaps other records may yet come to hand to resolve the matter finally.

30. *The first motor bus licensed (in June 1909) by Dunfermline Magistrates was this 15-seat Arrol-Johnston, owned by George Scott of Culross. Mr Scott is seen sitting beside driver Alex McKenzie, being shown how to drive his new vehicle.*

George Scott lived in Bishop's House, Culross, now one of the properties owned by the National Trust for Scotland; prior to his move into motor bus operations he ran brakes, cabs and landeaux. He was contractor for the Royal Mail, announcing his coming in time honoured fashion by use of a long brass horn kept when not in use in a basketwork case. Later the family moved to Dunfermline and during World War I ran a bus to Rosyth. Mr Scott retired in 1922 and with no family interest in the business it was wound up and the effects and vehicles auctioned.

The same fate did not befall his close rival, Tom Cousins. Tom had been employed as a horse-bus driver with Herdman of Culross, whose business he acquired early in 1901. The first motor buses were purchased in association with his brother John, and a younger brother Matthew (Matt) worked with Scott for a time before joining his brothers. Over the ensuing years a large number of buses passed through their hands — several Scottish built Halleys being used in early years. Routes were expanded and eventually High Valleyfield and Blairhall were served and the Culross 'main' route extended as far as Alloa in June 1921.

Another pre-world War I motor bus operator in the Dunfermline area was William Philp of St Margaret Street, a long established horse-bus proprietor operating originally to Lochgelly, then to Kelty, and also to Steelend. His first motor bus was obtained in September 1911, a 28-seat Straker-Squire charabanc with which a service was started to

31. *The second motor bus licensed (on the same day as that opposite) was a 10- seat Albion — seen here outside the Culross garage of Thomas Cousins.*

32. *These old buildings in Culross are now owned by the National Trust, but were not so prized in 1913 when this scene was recorded. Two of Cousins' buses are on show; his garage was on the right — just out of the photo.*

33. *By 1914 William Philp owned the largest fleet of motor buses licensed in Dunfermline — five vehicles. Two of his Commers (SP 1154 and V 1597 behind) are seen on a hire near Donibristle. Running repairs were being made to the engine.*

Charlestown via Limekilns. In 1914 one of his vehicles, a Commer, was requisitioned by the Army for war service. The business appears to have been given up about January 1917 and the assets may have been acquired by the West Fifeshire Motor Service Co which operated from premises in James Street, Dunfermline, (Philp's rear yard). By March 1917 West Fife was running to Charlestown, Saline and Steelend, all routes which had latterly been served by Philp. Just a few months later, in December 1918, this Company ceased operations, 'owing to the cars being under repair resulting from the deplorable state of the roads'.

By the start of World War I three West Fife operators had ventured into motor transport – Scott, Cousins and Philp. Wilson's horse-bus to Inverkeithing continued until about 1915, probably the last in the area.

The outbreak of war in August 1914 caused many plans, including those for tramway extension, to be suspended. A bus service was not capital intensive and therefore had obvious attractions. On 19 September 1914 Dunfermline Council approved a service by a new company, the Auto-car Bus Company (ABC) operating from a garage in Baldridgeburn. They had intended a Dunfermline to Kirkcaldy route but in fact commenced with a four times a day run from Dunfermline to Kelty via Kingseat. This was immediately popular, linking the towns by the direct route while the tram journey required a change of cars at Cowdenbeath Fountain. Tram takings on the Kelty route dropped immediately by nearly £8 per week (nearly two thousand penny fares).

By 1915 the ABC's Kelty run was hourly, with in addition a summer Sunday Aberdour service, single fare 9d. During July 1915 services were commenced from Dunfermline (Abbot Street) to Inverkeithing and to Rosyth, hourly. The latter route served the construction works for the new Naval Dockyard (to which special trains for workers were also run).

In November 1915 ABC was registered as a limited liability company, 'to purchase the business carried on by John Chisholm and George Jack under the style of the Auto-car Bus Company, otherwise known as the ABC Bus Company'. (These names will feature again.) The date of transfer was 28 June 1915, two buses being then owned. Share capital was £2000, the two principals becoming directors, issuing themselves £500 each in shares for the undertaking. A third director was Macneill Robson, 'Motor Representative'.

The company purchased new vehicles – a Lothian (designed and constructed in Edinburgh by the Scottish Motor Traction Company), plus some Caledons, manufactured in Glasgow. Carrying workers to and from Rosyth proved lucrative and the separate Inverkeithing service was dropped, with instead a connecting run from Rosyth (Castle Gates) to Inverkeithing. As war-time conditions worsened, restrictions on petrol supplies were imposed from July 1916 and the Kelty run was discontinued (other than at weekends). When in May 1918 the tramway to Rosyth opened, taking the bulk of Naval Base traffic, the ABC withdrew their service, concentrating instead on the direct Inverkeithing operation. Kelty was again run daily from June 1918. All was not well behind the scenes, however, as Dunfermline Council were attempting to levy a 3d per mile tax for road use. The Company in turn appealed to the Secretary of State. Eventually, on 3 July 1918 ABC was purchased by Alex Sturrock and John McGregor of Kirkcaldy, proprietors of the General Motor Carrying Company which had operated buses from Kirkcaldy since 1913. The new owners quickly wound up ABC which ceased operation in August 1918; some of the vehicles may have passed to GMC. The final meeting of ABC creditors was held in Glasgow on 2 September 1918.

34. *It is believed that this early Argyle wagonette was used in pre war years to provide a feeder service to the trams from West Wemyss.*

The coastal industrial area around and east of Kirkcaldy was well served by the tramway systems. The first motor bus recorded in the area was that operated from November 1909 by Mr Burnett between Largo and Kennoway via Leven. This was referred to in a contemporary report as a 'large motor bus' – but no details are known of the operator or the duration of his enterprise.

Messrs Smith and Williams of Commercial Road, Leven started a service on 2 October 1913 using a 30-seat charabanc, competing with the Wemyss trams between Leven and East Wemyss. The first run was marred, as reported, '. . . a piece of carelessness saw water instead of petrol being put into the tank, and much time was wasted stripping down the carburettor'! This venture was not a success; the trams more than held their own, and the bus was withdrawn without notice.

In Kirkcaldy the first regular bus operator was James Tod, lemonade manufacturer, who at weekends put charabanc bodies on to his Albion lorries – mostly for private hires although he operated for a short time in 1914 regular services between Kirkcaldy and Markinch.

July 1913 saw the formation of what was quickly to become Fife's largest bus operator, the General Motor Carrying Co, based initially at 25 Thistle Street, Kirkcaldy. Brothers-in-law Alex Sturrock and John McGregor ran a haulage business in Kirkcaldy and Leith for J & J Todd, flour millers. On Saturdays and Sundays, to fully utilise their vehicles, the lorry bodies were swopped for charabanc seats, and originally used for touring and private hire.

The first regular stage service commenced during July 1913, from Kirkcaldy (West Bridge) tram terminus to Kinghorn and Burntisland. This proved immediately successful and in September a second route from Kirkcaldy (Nicol Street) to Kinglassie via Cardenden was inaugurated, followed a month later by a Mondays only trip from Kirkcaldy (Gallatown) to Thornton. The first buses were Commers but as the fleet expanded many purchases were the Glasgow built Caledons, memorable for their high fluted radiators carrying the blue and white Saltire. The vehicle livery was 'Rover Grey' and the buses were kept immaculate, the conductor being responsible for sweeping out the bus each time it reached a terminus. Initially buses were named after castles – there were the 'Dunnikier Castle', 'Seafield Castle', 'Ravenscraig Castle', 'Balwearie Castle', 'Rossend Castle', 'Wemyss Castle', and probably others but as the fleet expanded numbers became more practical if less exotic.

On 18 December 1913 a major advance was the inauguration of a seven-mile service from Nicol Street to Lochgelly by Cardenden and Auchterderran, immediately successful.

36. *The terminus of the first GMC route was here at Harbour Place, Burntisland. The railway bridge behind was built for the line connecting to the Forth Railway Bridge in 1890. The bus is a solid-tyred Caledon, registration S 7950, fleet Number 14.*

The outbreak of war saw suspension of the Kinglassie and Thornton runs although Burntisland and Lochgelly continued, and another popular route from Nicol Street to Leslie via Thornton and Markinch commenced on 9 September 1914. In 1915 the fleet num bered eight vehicles. Petrol shortages dictated that frequencies were less than adequate with much overcrowding, and some of the buses were converted to run on town gas, carried in large canvas bags on the roof.

In Dunfermline at this time James Beattie, proprietor of a fish and chip cart (!) obtained a bus which also ran on town gas, and was licensed to operate to Charlestown. In May 1917 Dunfermline licensed seventeen motor buses (Cousins 4, ABC 9, West Fife 2, McEwan 1 and Scott 1). At this time, from Kirkcaldy, only GMC were providing motor bus services. The tramways continued during the war years, with conductresses taking the jobs of men who had gone to fight.

John Chisholm, co-founder of ABC, was in March 1919 granted a licence as 'Chisholm's Motor Service' to Limekilns and Saline, following withdrawal of the West Fife Motor Service Co which had until February served these villages. Chisholm soon acquired a new partner, James Brand Jnr, and from October 1919 started operating from Dunfermline to Kelty via Kingseat, the partnership trading as the 'Saline Motor Service'. Soon adverts referred to the 'famous grey charabancs, 14, 29 and 34 seaters available for hire'. The first bus was a Halley, then came Karriers, and as the fleet grew, AEC's were added.

In Fife, as elsewhere in the country, development of the motor bus industry took a much more positive direction after the First World War. Many ex-Army vehicles and chasses were released and numerous operators started local routes. Some prospered and expanded, others did not. Some had ambitions, others were content to run one bus on one route. Many villages and towns had their local operator but some Companies with aspirations grew to serve the highways and byways of Fife. Through these years the bus industry in Fife developed simultaneously in the centres of population, and operations grew separately in Dunfermline, Kirkcaldy, East Fife, Cupar and North Fife. As these areas developed through in the twenties it may be justified to deal separately with development in each.

37. *Dunfermline car 19 fighting its way through snowdrifts on its exposed 'cross-country' route. Manpower and shovels had to be resorted to – the snowplough on the tram inadequate on this occasion.*

Dunfermline District

Dunfermline District, as defined by the Local Authority (Scotland) Act 1974, includes the Royal Burgh and the surrounding West Fife area, Lochgelly and as far east up the coast to include Aberdour.

Bus industry records are mostly ephemeral but Dunfermline Town Council exercised their responsibilities by the issue of omnibus licences and later attempted to bring a degree of control by imposing bus Bye-Laws. Fortunately some of these records still exist. In 1920 licences were granted for sixteen motor buses used by four operators (Scott, McEwan, Chisholm and Cousins). By 1922 licences were issued numbering no less than fifty-nine to vehicles operated by sixteen operators; in 1924 for eighty-two vehicles by twenty-one operators; the following year one hundred and ten bus licences were issued – after this the situation becomes more complicated as Fife County then also started issuing licences. The number of vehicles operating increased rapidly with, in the last year of issue prior to the implementation of the Road Traffic Act – 1930 – four hundred and two bus licences were issued by Dunfermline Council – but these were now consolidated to just ten operators.

The year 1921 was when many would-be entrepreneurs took up perceived opportunities, opening up routes to the hinterlands. By then Bisset & Gilmour (Chemists and lemonade manufacturers) of Burntisland had established a regular service, James Beattie ran to Limekilns and Saline, then operated with an Albion charabanc to Aberdour. George Jack operated a 30-seat Karrier also on the Aberdour run, competing with Wm H Robinson (a Ford and an Albion). Thomas Sked started a run to Steelend from August 1921, Tom Turnbull got authority for a 14-seater running to Cowdenbeath, and Thomas Harrison ran from Dunfermline to Kingseat. Soon Turnbull extended his run to Lochgelly.

One of the early Companies which was to make a major contribution to the West Fife bus scene was the Kelty Motor Transport Co, whose proprietors William Milne and William McLean started a Dunfermline (Inglis Street) to Kelty by Kingseat and Lassodie run from late 1921. Kelty – a mining community of some 2500 souls – was soon able to boast no less than four bus operators! The immediate loser from this activity was the tramway which struggled on, losing money, for several years until discontinued after October 1931. Kelty Motor Transport (KMT) opened a second route from Cowdenbeath (Fountain) to Milnathort from 22 June 1922 and operated a smart fleet of dark green Leylands. Liveries were now becoming more important for distinguishing between possible competing operators on the same route – previously in many instances the vehicles would run in whatever paint style the body-builder had in vogue.

39. *William Philp's third motor bus seen in Saline Main Street, probably in the summer of 1913. Its arrival has attracted a deal of interest in the peaceful village; Note that most of the boys are barefoot.*

Operators serving Dunfermline in 1922 were: to Charlestown, James Beattie (1 vehicle licensed) and William Robinson (3 vehicles); to Burntisland and Aberdour, Bisset & Gilmour (3), Alex Blyth (1), George Jack (1); to Culross (also Alloa, Blairhall and Crombie), T & J Cousins (12); to Saline, Augustus (Gusty) Factor (1), Charles Hendry (1) and the Saline Motor Service (8) which also operated to Inverkeithing, Aberdour and Kelty; to Kingseat and Lassodie, Thomas Harrison (2); to Lassodie and Kelty, Kelty Motor Transport (2); to Cowdenbeath, Penrose and Law (2) and John Turnbull (1); to Inverkeithing, George Scott (1); to Valleyfield, William Smith (1); and to Kirkcaldy, the General Motor Carrying Company (19). Several differing stances were used in the town, St Catherine's Wynd for Aberdour, Burntisland and Charlestown; Pittencrieff Street for Culross, Blairhall and Valleyfield; Pilmuir Street for Saline, Steelend and Inverkeithing; Inglis Street for Cowdenbeath and Kelty; and Park Gates (Appin Crescent) for Kirkcaldy.

The situation can already be seen to be less than satisfactory, and was only to deteriorate as even more operators appeared on the scene. David Gold in 1922 started on the Cowdenbeath service, the Rosyth Motor Co (Messrs Weir and Penman) to Rosyth and Aberdour. A new name appeared, running initially from Dunfermline to Inverkeithing from 8 March 1923. This was Frank A Simpson (a former driver with Cousins, also West, and Saline MS), who was to make a major impact on the Fife bus scene. From his Market Street base he extended to reach Aberdour, then Burntisland. By this time the Burntisland

38. *Car 11 heading along Lower Oakfield, Kelty, probably when the line was newly opened in November 1910, judging by the interest being aroused all round.*

route was also being contested by Bisset & Gilmour and the Saline MS. After a time of unrestrained competition, Fife's first co-ordinated service was arranged with the three proprietors 'amicably' dividing the timetable from April 1924.

At this time the Tramway Company still saw itself as the first, and foremost, provider of local transport, with a large amount of capital invested in plant and equipment – a commitment which the upstart bus interloper did not have to match. The tramways were spending large amounts of money on new track to do away with the delays inherent in the original single track and loop layout. Along with this investment in the trams they saw a parallel need to meet the competition of the unrestrained volume of motor bus opposition. For many years the tram route from Dunfermline through Crossgates, Cowdenbeath and Lochgelly to Lochore had resisted

competition, but in May 1922 bus opposition started and quickly mushroomed. Soon total chaos prevailed. Bus operators chased the trams, themselves and all available fare-paying passengers. Although industry in Fife in general was in a depressed state and mining in particular in severe recession, people had to be mobile to chase available work; to save a halfpenny or a penny on a journey was important, also to a bus operator, to make a penny was vital – so much so that it was not unknown for a bus approaching its destination, the driver spying a profitable queue waiting for the return trip on the other side of the road, to summarily eject his remaining passengers and do a swift U-turn and load up for the return trip. Last run at night was also, if only sparsely patronised, liable to 'break down' before the terminus and miraculously be restored to life as soon as the disgruntled ex-passengers had disappeared from sight (on foot)!

 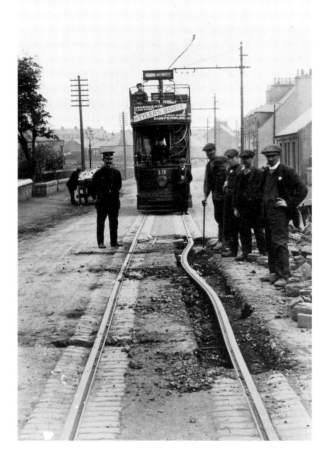

40, 41. *These photographs illustrate the problems induced in the tram track from mining subsidence. Car 22, on the left, is on the reserved track line leading to Kelty, unable to negotiate the chicane. Car 13 in the other scene is just west of the Cowdenbeath depot. Note the youthful conductor and the very resigned lady passenger on the top deck.*

The Tramway Company's reaction was to place in service five Tilling-Stevens petrol-electric buses (with the petrol engine driving an electric motor which in turn drove the rear wheels by a chain drive – and with an accelerator which was almost like a tram controller varying the power through the motor). This type had also been adopted as standard by the associated Scottish General Omnibus Company (the former bus department of the Falkirk Tramways Co).

The 'Tram-Bus' operators (The Tramway Bus Dept) applied in February 1924 to operate to Burntisland but were advised that this route was sufficiently provided for, but they were instead granted licences to run to Valleyfield, Culross and Kincardine. The following month they were given licences for Rosyth and Inverkeithing, on the basis that these were to determine potential traffic for the long-planned tramway to connect these areas. Also granted were licences to run to Limekilns and Charlestown. When the first buses arrived, two routes were inaugurated on 3 April 1924, serving Inverkeithing, and Burntisland via Aberdour. This was in direct opposition to the wishes of Dunfermline Magistrates and immediately put the 'Tram-Bus- in a state of conflict, not only with the Magistrates but also, and more publicly, into conflict with the existing operators, Bisset & Gilmour, Saline MS and Frank Simpson. Blyth had disappeared from the scene – indeed his licence *may* have been used by the 'Tram-Bus'

to cover their operations. George Jack who had operated on the Aberdour run in 1921 had by this time sold out to David West, who had previously been a Saline MS driver. Jack had been a driver with ABC, but he allowed his bus operations to lapse, concentrating instead on road haulage – a business which continues today. The Aberdour run was even more keenly contested on summer weekends. The large numbers of day trippers required buses to be drawn from other routes, running from Dunfermline, Lochgelly and Kirkcaldy. The three main operators divided up operations, but the theory was more successful than the practice – racing, poaching and hair-raising driving on the unmetalled roads with solid tyred vehicles perhaps proved thrilling to the crews but less so to their shaken, dust-covered passengers!

The first long distance service from Dunfermline was by James Beattie, to Perth from September 1922, using on Sundays the bus which normally plied to Charlestown, but this appears to have been short lived. It is unfortunately the case that many bus services, started with a well publicised flourish, disappeared the scene without any public comment. It was to be some years before such a lengthy regular service was again attempted.

Competition on the tram route has been mentioned. The first to challenge for traffic on the main Dunfermline-Cowdenbeath-Lochgelly artery was Robert Scott, of Park Avenue, Cowdenbeath, followed quickly by

42. *Seven of the 'Tram-Bus' fleet of Tilling-Stevens buses photographed at Beverkae Crossroads on a children's outing in 1925 from Cowdenbeath to Donibristle.*

A & A Young of Kelty who had eighteen months earlier operated a (for the time) lengthy route from Kelty to Kirkcaldy via Cowdenbeath (reversing) and Lochgelly. Alex Young who founded this Company started operation with two ex-Army chassis, both of which had charabanc bodies and were used for touring; the first was a Maudsley, the second a Guy. Both charabanc bodies were from Crerar of Crieff. Young's first service bus is said to have been a model 'T' Ford to which he fitted the body of the horse brake which had been run by Sandy McEwan. With this contraption he ran from Dunfermline to Lassodie Rows, a service which he passed – with the Ford – to J & J Ramsay (of Lassodie) in 1923.

One of the best known, and largest, of the local bus operators lost its identity during 1925. T & J Cousins, with sixteen buses operating to Culross, Crombie, Alloa, High Valleyfield and Blairhall, was purchased by the Scottish General Omnibus Co, the date of transfer being 30 May. The Culross garage was sold and the vehicles absorbed into the SGO Co fleet, where they were given numbers 79-94. Several of these were transferred within associated companies and Halley charabanc SP4901, rebuilt, was later in the Wemyss Tramway's bus fleet, then finally with GMC Kirkcaldy.

A & A Young is the second of the Kelty bus owners to be mentioned; another, John Turner of Station Road ran originally (from June 1924) from Lochgelly to Wellwood and later Dunfermline to Lochore; finally, John Davidson of Black Road, from 1924 ran north to Kinross and Milnathort (later extending to Perth), and in 1926 joined the fray on the tram route. Davidson's business was acquired in

March 1928 by Young's. Turner, who themselves took over James Bernard of Dunfermline in September 1927, survived to be absorbed by Dunfermline Tramway's Omnibus department in October 1931.

The other Kelty operators, Young and KMT, in an endeavour to fight off larger combines, formed a loose association with Baxter of Cowdenbeath (another ABC) in May 1931, but despite this all three succumbed to Alexander's in September of that year.

But that is moving too far forward. Competition grew more and more fierce – and violent – on the Dunfermline to Lochgelly service until by 1926 no less than eleven operators were *officially* competing with the ageing tramcars (Young, Turner, John Brown, James Brown, Bernard, Mitchell, Scott, Davie (or Divito), Penrose, Peattie, and the 'Tram-Bus'). Dunfermline Council tried to enforce its omnibus byelaws – even to the purchase of two stopwatches 'to time the buses on the new section of Halbeath Road'. The new road incidentally had been greatly subsidised by the Tramways who had paid for new double track, and who had to maintain the width of the tracks plus 18 inches on either side (fifteen feet of the new width of forty feet). The competing buses obtained great benefit but paid nothing other than road tax and minimal licence fees.

Meetings were convened by the Dunfermline magistrates, to which the bus operators were invited, with the intention of achieving amicable introduction of the byelaws. These were inconclusive and it became necessary for Dunfermline to attempt to impose its timetables. The main difficulties related to the services to Burntisland and to Lochgelly and Lochore. With regard to the latter, the existing basic eight buses per hour frequency was proposed to be reduced to six buses; the peak 5-minute frequency (twelve buses per hour) was to be reduced to 15 minutes (four buses per hour) on weekdays, five minutes only on Saturdays. Timetables were drawn up 'in the interests of equity' to attempt to give each operator a fair share – the detailing of which must almost have required the wisdom of Solomon. (Licences were divided into three groups and weekdays divided into periods of one and a half days – on weekdays groups took their turns for a 15-minute service, at the weekend from 4 pm on Fridays all groups combined to give a 5-minute service up to

43. *Cousins' Halley SP 4901 had a long and varied history, passing first to Scottish General (where it is seen as their No 83), then to the Wemyss Tramways Co.*

TABLE I

Showing Groups and Starting Times of Omnibuses, Monday to Friday.
The last two columns show Weekend Times as explained in Table II

Minutes after hour	GROUP A		GROUP B		GROUP C			
	Starting from Dunfermline	Starting from Lochore	Starting from Dunfermline	Starting from Lochore	Starting from Dunfermline	Starting from Lochore	Weekend Times Mon.	Wed.
0	John Brown	Turner	Bernard	Young	Scott	Peattie	10	20
15	James Brown	Young	Penrose	Mitchell	Young	Brand	35	40
30	Scott	Mitchell	Scott	Young	Davie	Peattie	50	55
45	Dunfermline Tramway Co.	Dunfermline Tramway Co.	Dunfermline Tramway Co.	Dunfermline Tramway Co.	Dunfermline Tramway Co.	Dunfermline Tramway Co.	5	25

TABLE II

Showing allocation of day and a half periods to Groups and giving starting times for Omnibuses at weekends

	First Week	Second Week	Third Week
Monday 10 am to Tuesday 4 pm	Group A	Group C	Group B
Tuesday 4 pm to Wednesday last run	Group B	Group A	Group C
Thursday 10 am to Sunday last run	Group C	Group B	Group A
Friday 4 pm to Sunday last run	Groups A & B	Groups C & A	Groups B & C

On Friday after 4 pm the Group which started that morning will continue at same starting times. The Group which was allotted Monday of same week will start at 10, 35, 50 & 5 minutes past the hour and the Group which was allotted Wednesday at 20, 40, 55 & 25 minutes past the hour as shown in Table I. All will continue at these times throughout the weekend.

midnight Sunday.) This came into effect on 6 September 1926 when the arrangements were as above.

It has to be understood that this was to vary from week to week, also that the numerous operators were supposed to deploy their staff and vehicles elsewhere when not actually working to the timetable!

Needless to say such complications were impossible to implement or control, but nevertheless enforcement was attempted, with a test case against J S Penrose of Cowdenbeath, held to be in breach of the Bye-laws by plying for hire at a time not allocated. He was fined £2 (or twenty days imprisonment) but appealed to the High Court. Needless to say, having got this far the lawyers took over, suggesting that the Magistrates were acting outwith their powers under the Burgh Police (Scotland) Act 1892; that the Bye-laws were unreasonable and an unlawful restraint of trade. The bus operators attempted the restricted timetable only during the first week of September; thereafter they reverted to the 5-minute frequency, regardless of the stipulated times. Penrose's argument was that, since he owned only one bus, for three days per week he was prohibited from working, therefore restrained from lawful trade, this being outwith the powers of the 1892 Act. The High Court disagreed, upholding the validity of the Bye-laws.

James Brand was also crossing swords with Dunfermline Council over their refusal to grant a licence to operate on his own account on the Aberdour and Burntisland route, which they maintained was already adequately served. Brand, with John Chisholm, ran the Saline Motor Service until January 1926, when fierce competition from the 'Tram-Buses' on the Burntisland route forced it into liquidation. William Jackson, coachbuilder, of Mill Street, Dunfermline, kept the SMS operating as a going concern towards his claim on the company, probably for bus bodies supplied. In March 1928 he disposed of the remaining assets to the Scottish General Omnibus Company.

Mrs Philp of Dunfermline was a conductress on the SMS, and she recorded her thoughts on these days in verse:

When I worked on the Saline buses
    My driver was Jock Hunter:
We got on fine for a short time
    When I was his Conductor

We'd start frae yonder Abbey Gates
    And hear the folks a' shoutin',
'Hi, stop that bus, for that yin's oors,
    Tae hang wi' the Tilling Steven.

Then on oor A E C we'd rattle,
    First stop wid be Pitreavie,
Then on again the Scotsman flew
    Till he reached Inverkeithing.

Then oot he'd bang, his hair on end,
    His bunnet raised wi' temper,
Whit time are you supposed tae leave?
    I'll learn you tae remember.

When a' wis o'er and tempers cooled
    And Jock his pipe had lichted,
Away he'd set for Aberdour
    Wi' every passenger lifted.

The Tilling Steven followed up,
    An angry driver fuming,
'I'll sort Jock Hunter yet for this,
    The morn I'll drive the Pullman'.

James Brand's persistence paid off and he was eventually, in August 1926, allocated the runs on the Lochore route which had previously been operated by George Divito (whose bus was off the road after an accident). Divito then sold his business to Peattie Brothers of Glencraig, later in 1928. Brand then received the licence formerly with Forte of Lochgelly, whose only bus was off the road severely damaged after a crash with a tramcar at Glencraig. Forte's licence ultimately passed to Simpson's Motors, and Brand's operations passed to A & R Forrester in May 1928. John Chisholm then in June 1927 commenced 'Chisholm's Bus Service', Dunfermline to Burntisland, with a 20-seat Berliet (which he obtained from the Saline MS!) – much to the annoyance of his former partner James Brand Jnr, who had also applied to run this service but had been refused. On 24 October the luckless Mr Chisholm saw his bus burn out when standing at St Catherine's Wynd. Combustion of these petrol-fuelled buses was not infrequent. Fuel spillage saturated timber bodywork and sparks from ill-maintained engines or carelessly discarded cigarettes could do the rest. Bus garages were also frequently the scene of disastrous damage by fire – the GMC Co suffering more than once. One Fife bus was memorable – it ran with a concrete fire-resistant floor! Until Chisholm obtained another vehicle in January 1928 his runs were worked by Simpson's; this was his final fling, Simpson's taking over the goodwill shortly thereafter.

A new operator appeared on the scene from July 1926, Dougald Miller of the grandly titled (but less grand reality) 'The Mansions', Cairneyhill – operating Dunfermline to Culross by Cairneyhill, and Dunfermline to Steelend. His fleet of Albions was conspicuous in a red livery with tartan waistband. (This was not uncommon – the tartan was printed on paper strips glued and varnished to the bus body.) A joint service with the SGO Co started

44. *Peaceful 1924 scene on the 'Great North Road', from Queensferry to Perth, at Inverkeithing High Street. Saline Motor Services have brought out one of their charabancs (SP 9241) on what was – hopefully – a fine summer's day.*

in April 1927 from Dunfermline to Stirling via Kincardine. Miller's business was purchased by the SGO Co about June the following year but operated independently under the original fleetname until around April 1930.

The Tramway Company's 'Tram-Bus' service had the weight of big business behind it, unlike the one-man-and-a-bus nature of many other operations. The SGO Co/Tram-Bus management decided to ignore the licensing authorities and succeeded, frequently by heavy-arm tactics, in overcoming most competition. They could flood any route with buses and (temporarily) reduce fares to unrealistic levels. The licensing authorities refused to recognise the SGO Co but a string of petty fines was not an adequate deterrent. The SGO Co was operating — unlicensed — to Saline (with Ramsay), to Charlestown (with Simpson) and to Burntisland (with Simpson and the Saline MS until they were seen off).

THE SCOTTISH GENERAL OMNIBUS COMPANY LTD.
DUNFERMLINE AND DISTRICT TRAMWAYS COMPANY
[Omnibus Department]
CRERAR'S MOTOR SERVICES.

PLEASURE SAILINGS
ON
LOCH EARN
BY OUR LUXURIOUS
TWIN-SCREW STEAMER
"QUEEN OF LOCH EARN"
MUSIC ON BOARD
Commencing 1st JUNE, and during the summer months.
DAILY.   DAILY.   DAILY.
FOR FULL PARTICULARS SEE OVERLEAF

45. *Handbill from 1926.*

The boundary between SGO Co and the 'Tram-Bus' operations became very blurred and although two fleets of vehicles existed in theory, the liveries were the same (dark red) and the buses were soon numbered in one series. Management of the Tram-Bus operations was vested in the SGO Co from March 1926, although licences were issued to, and buses registered to the Dunfermline Tramways Company until 1931. Several vehicles obtained by the SGO Co by takeovers were incorporated in the Tramways bus fleet. Other one-man operators came (and sometimes quickly went) in attempts to break into the fiercely contested busiest routes — sometimes going off to lick their wounds and re-appear testing out another route elsewhere. Thomas Knox of Torryburn started a run to Alloa in June 1927; extended to Stirling in September, and after this short existence was bought out by the SGO Co in February 1928, the one and only bus put in the Tramways fleet. Knox went to Wick, where he operated the 'Pioneer' service to Thurso.

The first mention in Fife of the name Walter Alexander appears to be in a December 1927 application — refused — for a long distance Dunfermline to Glasgow licence. At this time Alexander's was a smaller Company than the SGO Co, operating mostly in Central Scotland.

From January 1928 the Burntisland route was operated by Simpsons MS and SGO Co/Tram-Bus alternately. A six-minute frequency was given on weekdays, increased to every four minutes at weekends (even then it was said that a 30-minute service was all that was required for the available custom). Extras were put on to Aberdour in fine weather.

46. *Dunfermline Tramway's Tilling-Stevens bus in Aberdour High Street, c1925.*

The first licence for long distance service passing through Dunfermline to St Andrews was granted in November 1927, to the Star Motor Service of Glasgow; to operate from Glasgow by way of Stirling, Alloa, Dunfermline, Kinross and Cupar. Before starting this long route Star was taken over by Peter Crerar of Crieff, to whom the licence passed in January 1928. Crerar was himself absorbed by SGO Co just two months later but again traded separately for some time. It does seem however that when the service eventually started in February it was run by Gilford coaches, still in Star's purple livery. On 10 December 1928 further long distance services started, operated jointly by the SGO Co and Kirkcaldy's General Motor Carrying Company (GMC). These were Lochore (!) to Glasgow and Kirkcaldy to Glasgow – how many Glaswegians wanted to book through to Lochore is not recorded.

47. *Alexander's Albion MS 7003 (No 21) at Lochore, about to embark on the lengthy Glasgow run.*

Another service to Dunfermline started in March 1928 by Crerar running from Crieff by Yetts of Muckhart, and in the same month James W Peter of Milnathort started operating Dunfermline to Dollar via Milnathort. At this time SGO was investing heavily in acquisition of small operators, and Hunter, operating to Kincardine, then later Miller of Cairneyhill, also running to Kincardine and westwards, were absorbed. Another rationalisation took place in November 1928 when licences held by Forte, Penrose and James Brown passed to Simpson's Motor Services.

During 1929 the Fife Tramway Light and Power Company promoted legislation to try to give a measure of protection to its tramway services in Falkirk and Dunfermline. They wanted – particularly after investing large

sums in track reconstruction – restriction on bus services on routes served by trams, plus protective fares, the buses having to charge higher fares. To their dismay the Commissioners of Inquiry found against and the protection sought was not granted.

This was the time for establishment of long distance, cross-country routes, with vehicles now able to compete for traffic with the railways. In April 1929 Cormie Brothers of Kirkcaldy were given licence by Dunfermline Magistrates for a new service linking Glasgow and Leven via Stirling, Dunfermline and Inverkeithing. A & A Young started a service from Dunfermline to Kelty via Wellwood and Gask which linked up with their existing Cowdenbeath to Perth via Kelty operation. Simpson's Motors from May 1929 started Kirkcaldy to Stirling; in the same month Kelty MT Co started Dunfermline to Cupar via Kelty, Kinross and Auchtermuchty (to St Andrews from July) while A & R Forrester of Lochgelly at the end of May started running Lochgelly to St Andrews, and Lochgelly to Dundee (actually to Newport where passengers transferred to the ferry boat).

A & R Forrester (Alex and Robert) had run the Transport Department of the Lochgelly Coal & Iron Co prior to establishing themselves as bus operators. Tours were operated before the establishment of a regular route from Lochgelly to Kirkcaldy in (it is believed) 1926, in competition with the established GMC. Routes to Kinross and St Andrews followed and from early days close associations were maintained with the then independent firm of Walter Alexander & Sons of Falkirk, with a number of vehicles purchased with Alexander built bodies from blocks of vehicles allocated to the Falkirk firm. On 1 October 1929 a new combine Simpson's and Forrester's was formed to amalgamate the businesses of Simpson's MS, Dunfermline and A & R Forrester, Lochgelly, creating a combined fleet of nearly sixty vehicles.

The Fife Tramway Light & Power Co, having seen the eclipse of its protectionist legislation, decided upon re-organisation. The considerably expanded bus side – which by now consisted of the Scottish General, the 'Tram-Bus', the Wemyss Tramways Bus Dept, the General Motor Carrying Company and all their associated and absorbed smaller companies – was sold off, leaving the FTL & P Co controlling power supply and tramways.

48. *The terminus in Kirkcaldy High Street of the service to Lochgelly. Leyland Lion FG 2894 started life in the fleet of Simpson's Motor Service, then was absorbed into Simpson's and Forrester's fleet in 1929, and passed to W. Alexanders in 1938 where it changed its identity from 'No 9' to 'L 86'.*

49. *Many bus photographs were recorded (fortunately for the historian) in Tay Street, Perth. Albion FG 5300 was purchased by A & R Forrester in July 1929, passed to Simpson's and Forrester's soon after as 'No 56', then became 'C 243' with Alexander in 1938. It was sold out of service the following year and had a further career as a lorry until 1948.*

By this time the national Railway Companies (the LMS and LNER in Scotland) had obtained powers to operate bus services, following dramatic loss of short distance revenue in the years after the First World War. To implement these new powers, instead of imposition of new companies on to the existing scene, the Railway Companies used their funds to buy up existing successful bus operators. The decision of the FTL & P Co directors came at the right time and the assets of the various companies were snapped up, and new directors implanted. For a while during the subsequent 'rationalisation' period each company maintained its identity. The main plank of the Railway Companies' activities was the Scottish Motor Traction Co of Edinburgh who quickly took a controlling interest in Walter Alexander & Sons. This latter Company became the main operational 'name' for the businesses acquired in Fife (although in mere terms of vehicles owned and route miles operated SGO Co probably exceeded Alexander in 1929), and eventually the 'Alexander' name was carried on almost every regular bus route in Fife.

After re-organisation the two main operating Companies in Fife were Simpson's & Forrester's, and GMC now trading as 'General', who between them by 1930-31 had seen off or purchased virtually every competitor. The independent operators who held out longest were Robert Scott & Sons, who sold out (with John Turner and J Mitchell of Kelty) ostensibly to the SGO Co in October 1931 – who re-licensed the buses under Dunfermline District Tramways.

The Tramway Company, after losing heavily on the Kelty run during the bus 'formative' years, eventually gave up the unequal struggle, the last tram running from Cowdenbeath to Kelty on 26 October 1931. This did not however indicate that the directors of the Fife Tramway Light & Power Co were giving consideration at this time to abandonment of tram operations. Although Fife's other tramways, Kirkcaldy and Wemyss, had ceased operation in May 1931 and January 1932 respectively, the FTL & P Co considered that they had too much recent investment in new track to simply write it off. The Dunfermline tramcars themselves were not replaced with modern vehicles (as were those of the Falkirk tramways). This decision was forced upon the Company as the original 1905 Falkirk cars

were totally worn out by the mid 1920s, also Dunfermline's car fleet was considerably in excess of that required for normal day to day service. Spare capacity followed from the closure of Kelty and from the Rosyth route which never did require the use of the fifteen new cars purchased for it in 1918. The Dunfermline trams, although perhaps looking ancient compared to the new Pullman buses, nevertheless kept their share of traffic, particularly between Dunfermline and Lochgelly. In the mid 1930s the trams were being used by over seven million passengers annually, and were profitable, returning regular dividends. It was only when the SMT group, not appreciative of these figures which represented loss of bus earnings, acquired the tramway interests of the FTL & P Co and closed the tramway on 6 July 1937, that the monopoly was finally achieved; Dunfermline's passengers left without choice for the next fifty years. From 1938 Fife's distinctive Simpson's & Forrester's and General buses were absorbed completely into the Alexander fleet, although still retaining an 'Area' identity within the consolidated company. This was found to be unwieldy and in 1961 the holding Company was split into three, with W Alexander & Sons (Fife) Ltd assuming responsibility for virtually every bus service originating in the County. The major recent change has been de-regulation of the bus industry in 1986 with the re-emergence of competition on a scale such as has not been witnessed since before the 1930 Road Traffic Act. Fife Scottish – the local constituent of the Scottish Bus Group – had to compete with Rennie of Dunfermline Ltd until 26 April 1990, when in an action reminiscent of the thirties Rennie suddenly withdrew virtually all of their stage services.

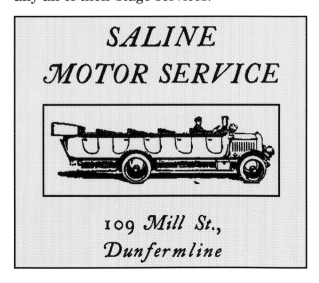

Kirkcaldy District

So far only services around Dunfermline have been considered; throughout the County similar, parallel, developments occurred.

In Kirkcaldy prior to World War I only two motor bus proprietors have been recorded, Sturrock & McGregor, whose General Motor Carrying Co has been mentioned earlier, and J M Tod. Proprietor of Seafield Tower Aerated Water Works, Tod owned a lorry to which he had a body added by a local joiner/coachbuilder, William Hunter. In November 1914 Tod intimated the start of a regular service to Markinch, but his timing could not have been much worse and the operation seems to have folded within weeks. Tod did purchase another Albion but probably used it only for touring hires. The other early operators in East Fife have already been mentioned, Burnett in November 1909 operating briefly from Largo to Kennoway, and Smith and Williams whose Leven to East Wemyss service started on 2 October 1913 but ended shortly after, their one charabanc doing tours and private hire only thereafter.

GMC had thus a virtual monopoly of services radiating from Kirkcaldy, and through World War I operated to Burntisland, to Lochgelly, and to Leslie via Thornton and Markinch. Business quickly picked up after the end of the War and in July 1918 Sturrock and McGregor purchased the Autocar Bus Company of Dunfermline. It was not retained as a going concern – perhaps they only wanted the vehicles. Further development saw the GMC being registered as a Limited Liability Company on 1 December 1919. The directors named were Alex Sturrock and John, James and Alex McGregor, and the capital was £20,000 in £1 shares. The two founders were paid £16,000 in shares for the business as a going concern. A subsidiary, Scottish Utility Motor Co, was incorporated at the same time to act as vehicle dealers, car hirers, and general carriers. Many GMC vehicles passed through this Company to be re-sold or re-constructed as commercial vehicles. It is thought that they may also have acted as agents for sale of Caledon chassis. Dundee coal merchant George Will started services to Alyth and Tealing and when he got into financial difficulties Sturrock and McGregor bought over his Will Motor Transport Co Ltd and took his vehicles (Caledons) into the GMC fleet. The WMT business was then wound up.

51. *The 'Wast Brig' was Kirkcaldy Corporation's appointed terminus for buses, where passengers had to transfer to the trams.*

As has been described when considering Dunfermline, the immediate post-war period saw a massive expansion in road passenger transport around Kirkcaldy – but not in the town, as Kirkcaldy Town Council prohibited operation of buses within the Burgh boundaries, to protect the interests of their tramways.

Probably the first new operator to appear in this post-war period was the Caledonian Motor Carrying Co (the 'Caley') which evolved from an old posting establishment run by Robert Andrew out of the Caledonian Hotel stables in Level. After his retiral in April 1920 the business was acquired by John Dewar who formed a limited company. Operation of one route from Leven to Anstruther via Largo and Colinsburgh was followed eighteen months later by Leven to Kennoway via Windygates, and then, from November 1923, by a Leven to Gallatown via East Wemyss service which of course paralleled the Wemyss tramway. This incensed the Tramway Company, particularly by the poaching tactics adopted by the bus drivers, who could nip in and out in front of the tramcars, lifting passengers waiting at the stops. To overcome this the Tramway Company introduced their own buses, then in April 1925 purchased a controlling interest in the 'Caley'. The Caley continued its separate existence, but only for private car hire.

The major expansion of the GMC Co took place in 1921, with the Burntisland route extended to Aberdour from June, followed by opening of new routes to Auchtermuchty via Falkland; to Windygates via Milton and Coaltown of Balgonie; and for a month only, to Pitlessie via Freuchie and Kingskettle.

Next to mount a major challenge to the Wemyss tramways – after the 'Caley' – was James Anderson of Buckhaven who (with brother Tom) became recognised as the prime 'chaser' of the Wemyss trams; his service started in May 1922 and attracted much custom. From November 1923 his operations were known as Buckhaven Motor Carrying Co, running chocolate-coloured Reos – much nipper than the trams, and a constant source of irritation to the tramway operators. The Andersons joined forces in April 1926 with James Roden, a local cinema owner who found here a profitable enterprise looking for expansion capital, and the undertaking re-formed as A & R Motor Services (Buckhaven) Ltd. Control of this new company was taken over just thirteen months later by the Wemyss Tramways Co, but it continued trading nominally separately until acquired by W Alexander & Sons Ltd on 20 June 1930 along with all the other subsidiary bus companies owned by the Wemyss organisation.

The benefits of bus operation were not lost on the Wemyss Tramway directors, who purchased their first three Tilling-Stevens petrol electric buses (the same type as were adopted as standard by the SGO Co and Dunfermline Tramways) in July 1922. Initially they ran along the roads parallel to the tramway, to try to drive off the 'chasers', but the Tilling-Stevens were slow and ponderous compared to the sprightly opposition vehicles. Nevertheless regular services were soon being run along the coast from Gallatown (later from Sands Road – the Esplanade) to Largo and Anstruther. Ultimately Wemyss buses reached as far afield as Glasgow, Perth and St Andrews.

52. *Road construction at Aberhill in the twenties, with one of Smith's Reos edging past.*

The financial backing of the Tramway Company was through the Balfour Beatty group which controlled the Fife Tramway Light & Power Co and all its subsidiaries. When the effects of unrestrained bus competition were most critically felt, decisions were made which anticipated those of the Railway Companies in 1930-31. In February 1926 therefore a controlling interest in the General Motor Carrying Co was purchased in the name of the Wemyss Tramways, with two Wemyss directors put on to the GMC board to replace Angus and James McGregor. Thereafter GMC was nominally a Wemyss subsidiary but independence of management (the two founders still very much in control) continued until eventually the cuckoo greatly outgrew its parent.

An interesting development in 1924 saw the GMC principals acquiring an interest in the Gala Motor Transport Co of Galashiels. This Company had been formed by Robert Wilson, who later moved to Carnwath to found a separate bus undertaking which is still a well respected bus and coach operation. Some interchange of vehicles follows – GMC buses going to Gala simply had the 'C' changed to a 'T'.

The GMC route to Perth (started in December 1927) put it into competition with the small business of Stanley Fuller of Newburgh who had inaugurated a regular run from Newburgh to Perth in May 1923. Fuller and GMC ran a joint Kirkcaldy to Perth run for a short time but he soon succumbed and his business and vehicles were absorbed into GMC from July 1928, although it continued to operate under the Fuller name for a few months. The garage at Newburgh was taken over and most of the employees retained.

In 1929 Alex Sturrock took an interest in the Glen Motor Transport Co of Fraserburgh (which also traded as 'General'). The convoluted nature of the motor bus industry of the time is shown by Gala Motor Transport also owning shares in 'Glen' – as did Robert Wilson as an individual also!

GMC's monopoly on profitable routes did not go unchallenged. Operators who competed on the coast road to Burntisland included David Glendinning of Kinghorn who set up in September 1923, and Harrow & Stocks, of Invertiel Road, Kirkcaldy, who survived from 1926 to be taken over by GMC in December 1930.

Another Company which owed its origins to chasing the Wemyss trams for passengers was Smith's Motor Service, of Ravenscraig Street, Kirkcaldy. Founded by J R Smith who had originally driven with the Autocar Bus Company of Dunfermline, he started with a Model 'T' Ford in 1923 but soon brought his brothers Tom, Dick and Harry into the business, each one driving a silver coloured Reo. A route was also run between Montrose and Forfar but this was taken over by the Cormie Brothers in July 1926. In Fife Smith's business expanded with routes to Leslie, to Auchtermuchty, then to Perth via Falkland, all competing with GMC.

On 21 December 1927 Smith audaciously set up the first bus service to run within the Burgh of Kirkcaldy. Kirkcaldy Council refused to sanction any bus operation within its boundary but Smith challenged this and within a month the Town Council acknowledged that they actually had *no* powers to prohibit unlicensed bus operation. This was a major climb-down, the significance of which was not lost on local bus owners and the scenes which had plagued the Wemyss Tramways five years earlier were soon repeated in the Lang Toun.

Smith's first town service – using buses boldly inscribed 'Kirkcaldy Motor Bus Service' – ran from Kirk Wynd to Gallatown via Bennochy Road, Den Road, Smeaton Road and Overton Road, covering residential areas away from the existing tram routes.

Mr Francis, Manager of Kirkcaldy's tramways, had just reported to the Council that not only should Parliamentary powers be (belatedly) applied for to regulate bus traffic, but also these be got to allow the Council to operate its own buses. The tram undertaking was considered a great municipal asset, contributing to the rates and still carrying over five million passengers annually. Kirkcaldy, he thought, was ideal for tramways – the saving in time by bus travel was considered negligible. There was, he considered, little requirement for extension to the suburbs as the Burgh had not then expanded much away from the tram routes. Francis recommended spending £100,000 on upgrading the tramways and doubling tracks between Junction Road and Gallatown – but that was all before Smith started their town bus service. In a supplementary report after that event he had to conclude that the tramways could no longer

53. *Very few photographs show Fife buses and trams together. This scene in Kirkcaldy High Street shows the ageing tram and the new bus – in this case Smith's Fiat GD 8848 and Corporation tram number 10. The differing proportions are remarkable.*

work profitably with the bus competition and that the only way they could retain control would be to run their own buses, paying 'bus wages', with girl conductors.

Cormie Brothers were next to seize the local opportunity, with from January 1928 a service linking Whytescauseway and Dysart via Mitchell Street, Dunnikier Road and Loughborough Road. Cormie's had operated buses in Aberdeenshire (to Tarland and Dunecht, which eventually passed to Alexander's in 1932) and from July 1926 also from Montrose to Forfar and to Bervie and Ferryden. These routes were sold to the Northern General Omnibus Co in December 1927 but two buses, a Halley and a Reo, were retained to open operations in Kirkcaldy.

These new services were immediately popular and yet another operator, Jack Brothers, entered the scene with a town service from Kirk Wynd to McIndoe Crescent. Where previously the established operators had been content to run through the town without taking short stage passengers, that now also changed, the immediate outcome being a drastic loss of revenue to Kirkcaldy's trams. This prompted a two-fold response: an immediate reduction in tram fares and an application for a Provisional Order to run the Corporation's own buses. Objections were lodged by the now established bus operators and the terms of the Order modified but by the time legislation was eventually enacted the damage was done, the buses established and the trams were on the way out.

Smith and Cormie both prospered, opening up several new routes. By the end of 1928 Cormie was operating from Leven through to Burntisland, extending during the following year to become Lundin Links to Aberdour. Eventually in January 1930 with a modern fleet of Maudslays and Crossleys Cormie inaugurated a 4-hour 'marathon' journey from Lundin Links to Glasgow, very popular at the Glasgow 'Fair' holidays when Fife became a mecca for many Glaswegians. Smith's operations were concentrated north of Kirkcaldy towards Perth – a route eventually shared more or less amicably with GMC. One of Smith's 'publicity stunts' was to raise funds for the Hospital Fete (prior to the NHS), when a 2d. bus service was run along the upper tram route from Gallatown to Whytecauseway. Total receipts ('less operating costs') were then handed over to the cause. It was to be run every month if sufficiently patronised but so far as can be established ran but once! Smith's operations succumbed to the blandishments of Alexander (in November 1931) when the routes and vehicles were passed over to GMC.

Cormie had higher ambitions. After the successful Glasgow operation and the continuing growth of traffic on the Kirkcaldy town route the brothers Cormie in October 1930 offered to purchase the Kirkcaldy tramways from the Town Council. Their offer of £20,000 for the by now decaying trams was rejected but only six months later the Council received an offer from Alexander's which was not treated in such a summary fashion. Cormie's were then subjected to intensive

54. *Smith's Ravenscraig Street premises; 1929. Driver J Webster, conductresses A Hynde, N Briggs and E Allan, plus assorted vehicles.*

competition on the long distance Glasgow route – mainly from Alexander. This followed a rejected take-over proposal from Alexander and after the Glasgow route was given up, from January 1931, Cormie concentrated on only one route, from Leven to Dunfermline. The brothers had constituted themselves as a Limited Company in November 1930 but this did not prevent acceptance of Alexander's offer on 11 October 1931, whereupon the vehicles were absorbed into Alexander's fleet and the Company put into liquidation.

As witnessed on the Dunfermline to Lochore route, a measure of shared timetabling was eventually agreed on the Kirkcaldy to Leven route between the operators, GMC, Wemyss and Smith. Fife County Council had observed the problems of unprincipled bus competition for some time and eventually created Bye-Laws for regulation – too little, too late. Overshadowed by proposed national control (which ultimately surfaced as the 1930 Road Traffic Act), local Bye-Laws were delayed for so long as to become unworkable. By now the Corporation tramways had lost much of their patronage and for the first time returned a considerable loss. It was recorded then that 'the cars clatter along like ill-favoured pit hutches and repairs are continually being made to track that is irreparable'. The repair shop at the depot was overcrowded with unserviceable cars, a consequence of their age and the state of the track. This was a period of great change in public transport in the Kirkcaldy area; ultimately the Council were forced to accept the inevitable, their tram routes under assail from Harris, Cormie, Smith, Brown, Houston, Scott, Ramage and

55. *'The Kirkcaldy Bus Problem' as seen by a local newspaper. Directing the traffic at the Adam Smith Halls junction has caused the over-development of the arms and hands of the points duty policeman. The tramcar is almost pushed out of the scene by the buses of (left to right) Messrs Forrester, G M C, A & R, Jack, Wemyss, Smith and Cormie!*

Hays. The firms which previously operated only outwith the town now competed for traffic amongst themselves and with the forlorn tramways, tied to their rails and delayed by track layout twenty years out of date.

Early in 1929 several bus owners got together to form the Scottish National Omnibus Company, hoping that strength from numbers would give them greater muscle for competition and a better bargaining position. The Fife firms involved were Cormie, Smith, Scott of Cowdenbeath and Peattie Brothers of Glencraig. It appears to have been a forlorn hope and the combine existed in nothing other than name.

During 1929 Kirkcaldy Magistrates licensed 305 buses operated by eleven separate undertakings; by now the town tramways were totally eclipsed. The manager, Mr Francis, was instructed to 'visit Wolverhampton or any other place to get information on up to date transport'. A sub-committee of the Council was formed to visit English bus and trolleybus operations. Tramway abandonment was in the air but a major difficulty was seen with the Wemyss Tramways having running powers over Kirkcaldy's tracks to Whytecauseway until 1941, although these had not been exercised for several years. Events now moved quickly and although a proposal was put forward for municipal trolleybus routes this came to naught. At a meeting convened in February 1931 to discuss the Wemyss through running question a surprise was sprung with the presence there of Baillie William Thomson of Edinburgh, the Chairman of the SMT Co, now the owner of W Alexander, GMC, Simpson's

and Forrester's and of course the Wemyss Tramways. By the end of the month a draft offer for the tramways undertaking was received in the name of W Alexander & Sons acting as SMT's subsidiary.

Alexander's offer was accepted unconditionally by the Council at the end of March. For the sum of £27,000 plus £2,000 per annum Alexander's undertook to provide 'the whole of the transport services in Kirkcaldy' after 15 May 1931. From that date the Corporation were to discontinue the tramway and restore the streets. The matter of the Wemyss through running was dealt with on the basis that since an offer for purchase of the Wemyss Tramways had been made cancellation of the agreement would be undertaken.

On the night of 15 May the Kirkcaldy trams made their last runs amidst large noisy crowds gathered to witness the event. The following morning a fleet of twenty single deck Alexander's Albion buses replaced the thirty-year-old trams. Six of the old cars found further use as shelters in public parks and eight were transferred to the Wemyss Tramways which continued for a few months to run from Gallatown to Leven. Bus services operated initially were: 1. Gallatown to Whytescauseway via the Upper Route, turning in the town along Park Place, Whytehouse Avenue and the High Street; 2. Invertiel Road – Pratt Street – High Street – Dysart; 3. Macindoe Crescent to High Street (Port Brae) via Overton Road, Smeaton Road, Den Road, Dunnikier Road and Coal Wynd; 4. Lina Street to High Street via Hendry Road, Forth Avenue, Park Gates and Nicol Street.

56. *Menu card of the Kirkcaldy tramwaymen's final meeting.*

Under the Road Traffic Act, bus regulation passed into the hands of Traffic Commissioners, who sat in Kirkcaldy for the first time in September 1931. Applications were heard from Cormie Brothers, GMC, Smith's Motors, Findlay Brown, A & A Young, Jack Brothers, Walter Alexander & Sons, J Hay and the Wemyss & District Tramways. The last named ran their trams until the end of January 1932. Control of the Wemyss Company had been acquired by the SMT monopoly in April 1931; thereafter vehicles were incorporated into the 'General' (GMC) although, as can be seen above, the name was certainly kept alive for licensing purposes for some time. The limited liability Company remained in existence until July 1938 when it was wound up in a tidying-up process which also saw the removal from the register of many other defunct bus companies.

Several of the names mentioned as appearing in the Traffic Commissioners' lists have not so far been referred to. James Harris of Commercial Road, Leven was in the first

57. *Fife's first double decker was Forrester's Leyland TD1 FG 5334. Seen in Hendry Road, Kirkcaldy, 1929.*

instance a taxi operator who acquired the touring charabancs of Robert Andrew in 1924. His first stage service commenced on 1 May 1928, from Kirkcaldy to St Andrews via Colinsburgh (this later became Buckhaven to St Andrews). The business of John Hay, Lundin Links, with a single route from Leven to Anstruther via Arncroach, was purchased c 1933 but it was not until 1 June 1939 that Harris became part of the Alexander empire. An earlier operator, based originally in Lundin Links, was David Ramage who, by December 1924, was running from Leven to St Andrews via New Gliston and Peat Inn, later extended to become Buckhaven to St Andrews. He, also, managed to resist Alexander's advances for some time, eventually capitulating in February 1936.

Landward eastern Fife was first served by David Eadie's Milton Motor Service based in Milton of Balgonie (by Markinch). With a 1921 Ford Model 'T' he started running a popular route from Leven to Leslie (Prinlaws) via Markinch. A Leven to Kinross service followed which was extended to Perth in May 1928. Still later a Kirkcaldy to Leslie route was added. His bright yellow fleet of immaculate vehicles, including several Thornycrofts, eventually totalled seventeen. Eadie's operations were purchased by Alexander in May 1932, the vehicles being absorbed into the GMC fleet.

The Windygates area was the base for two small local operations. Findlay Brown had a lorry with a charabanc body used at weekends for touring. With this a service was started, Windygates to Leven via Methilhill. One of his drivers, Joe Houston, branched out and with his father and brothers formed A Houston & Sons. With their first bus, a Model 'T' Ford purchased from Harry K Brown of Kirkcaldy, a service was started, also from Windygates to Leven but going via Inner-Leven. Houston extended his routes, reaching from Leven to Cuper via Montrave, and to St Andrews via New Gliston and peat Inn. A service also ran to Star of Markinch. Following the death of A Houston in 1929 the business, including six vehicles. was sold to Findlay Brown. This Brown, one of several Fife operators of that name, was by September 1931 running from Leven to Newport to meet the Dundee ferry with a smart fleet of Albions. His business passed to Alexander on 11 October 1931.

58. *The Shore, Anstruther was the starting point for Gardner's services. Three of his vehicles are together, that nearest the camera is ES 9739, purchased from Crerar of Crieff.*

North and East Fife

In the East Neuk of Fife the pioneer of bus operations was Tom Gardner of Harbourhead Garage, Anstruther. A charabanc for hires was purchased in 1922, a regular service linking Anstruther, Crail and St Andrews being introduced the following year. This was extended over the years to become Elie – Anstruther – Crail – St Andrews – Newport, then Leven to Newport by 1930. A St Andrews town service (Lomond Drive to Market Street) was run for one summer only but was not profitable and was not repeated. Gardner's business, with sixteen buses, was purchased by Alexanders in October 1931. Matt Gardner remained in charge as Depot Superintendent at the new (1927) garage until it was closed in 1982.

Mention of St Andrews brings one to realise that the University town had no local bus operator. Perhaps too small to justify an in-town service, Hamilton's had a 20-seat Lancia but it was only used for touring. In June 1923 Kirkcaldy's GMC started to operate from St Andrews to Crail and Anstruther. The buses for this service were driven up each day from Kirkcaldy until such time as a garage was built in Grange Road. A second service from St Andrews to Cupar via Blebo

and Strathkinness followed – these perhaps preventing the emergence of a local operator.

Cupar, County Town of Fife and centre of administration, was the base for several separate bus operators. The first touring charabanc in Cupar had been purchased early in 1920 by C M Grant of the Cupar Arms Garage, Burnside. Horse brakes had been operated from the hotel for many years, and a motor garage business available from 1914. The original small charabanc was joined by a 14-seat bus and from May 1921 regular operation started from Cupar to St Andrews via Dairsie and Guardbridge. Other services (some only one day a week) followed to Newport (for the Ferry), Springfield, Luthrie and Ladybank. Next in this particular field was Wm C Smith of the Crossgate whose first charabanc was purchased in July 1920. Tours only were run until September 1923, when, using the fleet name 'Central Garage', a route was inaugurated from Cupar to Kettlebridge via Ladybank (later extended to Falkland). Various other routes followed, some Market day or Saturdays only. Competition had been rife on the route to and from the Tay Ferry at Newport, Central Garage and Grant's indulging in all the cut-throat tactics which had been in evidence elsewhere in the Kingdom.

Cupar's third operator was Wm H Sharp of Crossgate, who started a run to Ladybank via Stratheden, Springfield and Letham, in 1924. This was extended to Ladybank and then Kingskettle and Elie. This route (and the business possibly) was taken over by Central Garage in April 1930, whereafter Grant operated the Ladybank service. The Central Garage business (with six buses) was purchased by SMT in June 1930 and operated thereafter as part of the Simpson's and Forrester operation. W C Smith was retained as the local manager.

A separate network of infrequent routes evolved on the north 'coast' of Fife, radiating from the Tay Ferry terminal at Newport. Robert Bayne ran to Tayport; George Collie ran to Wormit and Balmerino, and David Y Johnstone of Tay Street, Tayport operated from Newport to Tayport and on to St Andrews. This lasted until taken over by Alexander (on behalf of GMC) in April 1935.

Finally, John M Clow of Edenside, Guardbridge, ran a service from the Tay Ferry at Newport to St Andrews via Guardbridge, commencing operations in 1922. The route was latterly operated jointly with GMC but Clow managed to retain his independence until April 1935.

Fife never totally succumbed to Alexanders — there were always one or two independent operators, but these were mostly tucked away in corners operating school or industrial services. Williamson of Gauldry, in the years after World War II, operated on infrequent North Fife routes and has now joined forces with Moffat of Cardenden. This combined operation now has a base in Glenrothes New Town, competing for some stage carriage work.

In the southern part of the Region, Fife Scottish has had competition from Rennie of Dunfermline on many routes. Rennie was established after World War II and prospered on contract work plus one long public service route to Portsmouth (catering mostly for naval personnel). Competition between Rennie and Fife Scottish in the Dunfermline area for a time produced conditions which were reminiscent of the 'thirties and routes where bus provision greatly exceeded demand.

Deregulation of bus operation is now *fait accompli* and at the time of writing sell-off of the constituent eleven companies of the Scottish bus group (including Fife Scottish) is imminent. Fife's public transport industry is undergoing a period of great change. This will probably provide such a degree of interest to the observer as was generated during the formative years.

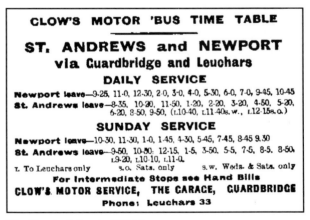

60. *Clow's Advert of 1930.*

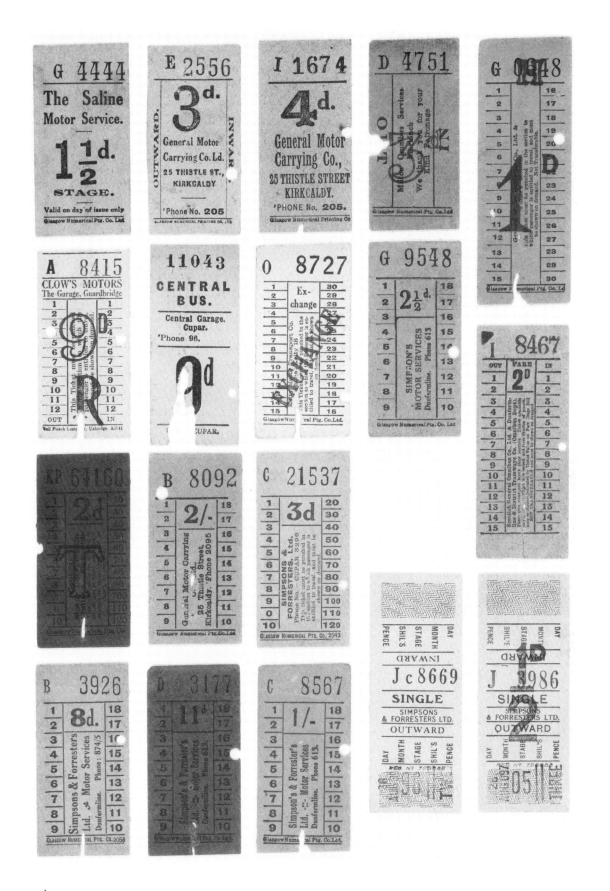

61. *Fife bus tickets, from top left.*
G 4444 Saline Motor Service 1½d salmon, E 2556 GMC 3d straw, I 1674 GMC 4d blue, D 4751 Milton MS 3d (blue overprint) on yellow, G 0648 GMC & Fullers joint issue 1d (red overprint) on green, A 8415 Clows Motors 9d (red overprint) on pale blue, 11043 Central Garage 9d white, O 8727 Kelty MT Co exchange (red overprint) on white, G 9548 Simpson's MS 2½d (red central imprint) yellow, I 8467 SGO Co and Dunfermline Tramways joint 2d grey, KP 64160 GMC 2d deep red, B 8092 GMC 2s 0d yellow, Simpson's & Forrester's Cupar 3d white, B 3926 Simpson's & Forrester's 8d straw, D 3177 11d orange, C 8567 1/- green. JC 8669 and J 3986 Setrite green and yellow respectively.

62. *The vehicles supplied by Alexander's to operate Kirkcaldy's tram replacement services, eighteen Albions plus, nearest to the camera, one Leyland, MS 9735. The Albions are, from the left, MS 8290, MS 7213, MS 8291, MS 8288, MS 8468, MS 7210, MS 7218, MS 8289, MS 7211, MS 8472, FG 2402 (ex Miller, Cairneyhill), MS 8071, MS 7216, MS 7217, MS 7214, VA 6474 (?), MS 8292 and MS 7215. Most of these were owned until 1930 by the Scottish General Omnibus Company.*

1. FIFE TRAMWAY OPERATORS

KIRKCALDY CORPORATION TRAMWAYS

Livery: Dark Bronze Green and Cream

First electric tramway system in Fife, and only municipally owned undertaking. Brought mobility previously unknown. Original route suffered from delays caused by single track construction. Town Council rejected plans for any motor-bus operation along its tram routes until this was challenged by several private bus operators. The trams could not compete and were abandoned on 15 May 1931, following an agreement with Alexanders that they would provide replacement bus services.

Routes:

    Link Street – Gallatown (from 28 February 1903)
    Junction Road – Whytescauseway or Park Gates (from 28 November 1903)
    Whytescauseway – Leven (joint with Wemyss tramways) from 14 November 1906 to 15 January 1917
    Junction Road – Dysart (from 26 January 1911)

Vehicles:

Cars	1-10	Built by Milnes 1902, 4-wheel double deck cars, reversed stairs
	11-22	Built by Milnes 1903-4, 4-wheel double deck cars, ordinary stairs
	23-26	Built by Hurst Nelson 1914, 4-wheel double deck cars, vestibuled platforms
		Eight cars to Wemyss Tramways 1931

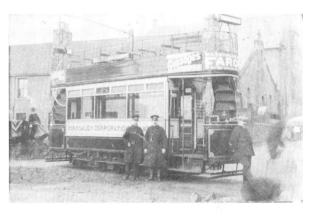

64. *One of the first trams at Cottage Hospital junction. Superintendent James Fisher leans nonchalantly on the front dash. Note the hearse on the left behind the car.*

63. *Inspector Kidd at Dysart terminus, showing car 6 at the 'end of the line', soon after opening of this extension.*

65. *Car 19 is in Links Street near the terminus. On the lamp-post can be seen the light signals which were supposed to control cars between passing places.*

66. *Early scene on the Wemyss Tramways at School Road, East Wemyss. Car 3 is attracting a great deal of interest.*

67. *The top of Leven High Street. The Leven Co-op butchers' department still has a tiled wall panel which shows a Wemyss tram in the High Street, a fine record of these early days.*

68. *Wemyss conductress with bogie car 17. Originally the side panels were removable, and seats were crosswise, but this was changed, the sides fitted permanently and longitudinal seating fitted. These big cars could not get round the sharp corners of the Kirkcaldy system and did not run beyond Gallatown.*

WEMYSS AND DISTRICT TRAMWAYS CO LTD

Livery: Wemyss Yellow, later Maroon and Yellow

Promoted by R G E Wemyss, transferred to private company. Opened 25 August 1906. Through operations into Kirkcaldy from 27 September 1906 to 15 January 1917. In 1912 Balfour Beatty took financial control, as part of their Fife Tramway Light and Power empire. Bus competitors after the First World War led to the Company starting its own bus services, eventually purchasing most of the major competition. Last tram ran 31 January 1932.

Routes:
    Leven to Kirkcaldy (Gallatown) via Methil and East Wemyss

Vehicles:

Cars		
	1-13	Built by Brush, 1906-1907, 4-wheel single deck cars with vestibuled platforms
	14-17	Built by Milnes-Voss 1907, 8-wheel single deck cars with vestibuled platforms
	18-19	Built by Brush 1925, 8-wheel single deck cars, sold to Dunfermline Tramways 1932
	20-21	Purchased from Potteries Tramways 1928, 8-wheel single deck cars with vestibuled platforms
	22-29	Cars purchased from Kirkcaldy Tramways 1931, rebuilt to single deck

69. *(left). Driver Bruce with his conductress and car 26 outside Cowdenbeath Depot, c 1926.*

70. *(right). Driver George Leighton and conductress Effie Adamson with car 30 at East Port, Dunfermline, terminus of cars to Cowdenbeath and points east. The decorations may be for the 1919 peace celebrations.*

DUNFERMLINE AND DISTRICT TRAMWAYS COMPANY

Livery: Bright Green and Cream

Tramways around Dunfermline built by a subsidiary of the Fife Tramway Light and Power Company (a Company within the Balfour Beatty Group). Despite considerable bus competition after World War I, a large investment was made in new double tracks to replace the original single line. An omnibus department was added in 1924, which through 'saturation' techniques gained control of several routes. The bus side was disposed of, but the trams continued until 5 July 1937 (except Kelty – closed 26 October 1931)

Routes:
    Dunfermline – Cowdenbeath (2 November 1909) Lochgelly (23 December 1909) Lochore (5 December 1912)
    Dunfermline – Townhill (3 November 1909)
    Cowdenbeath – Kelty (17 November 1910)
    Dunfermline – Rumblingwell (27 December 1913)
    Dunfermline – Rosyth (17 May 1918)

Vehicles:
Cars	1-43	Built by UEC Co 1909-1917, 4-wheel double deck cars
	44-45	acquired 1919 from Notts & Derby Tramways Co, 4-wheel double deck cars
	44-45	acquired 1932 from Wemyss Tramways Co, 8-wheel single deck cars

71. *The last of Fife's trams -- the Dunfermline cars lined up at Hill of Beath after abandonment of service on 4 July 1937.*

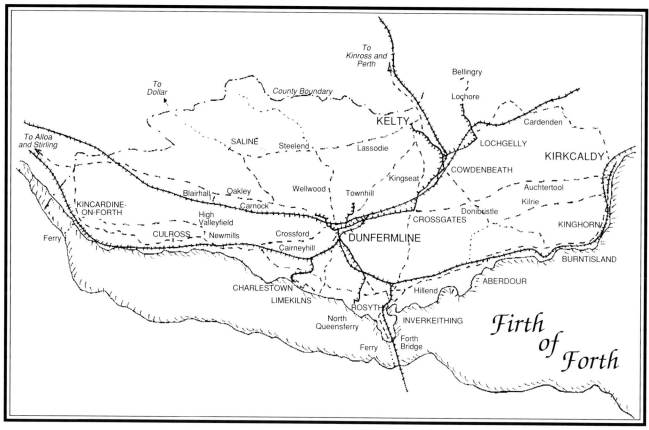

72. *Map of bus routes around Dunfermline.*

SIMPSON'S
Motor Service
'Phone 613

Unequalled for Touring

Our Luxuriously Fitted
Charabancs give you
Maximum Comfort and
Safety

TOURS DAILY

: Private Parties' Tours :
Arranged

1 Market Street,
DUNFERMLINE

1920s handbill.

CITY AND ROYAL BURGH OF
DUNFERMLINE.

Omnibus Byelaws

DRIVER'S LICENCE.

Bus driver's licence, issued by Dunfermline Burgh, 1928.

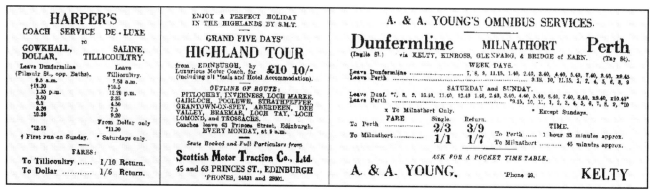

Press cuttings, July 1930.

2. BUS OPERATORS - WEST FIFE

ARNOTT Thomas Arnott, Venturefair Farm by Dunfermline

One vehicle licenced, May 1924 and May 1925
No detail of vehicle or route operated

AUTOCAR BUS COMPANY (ABC) LTD John Chisholm and George Jack, Rumblingwell by Dunfermline

Livery: Vermillion Lake and Cream

Established August 1914, first operated Dunfermline to Kelty via Lassodie from 19 September 1914. Became limited company in November 1915. Services curtailed by petrol use restrictions July 1916 and some vehicles converted to run on town gas. Control of company acquired in July 1918 by Sturrock and McGregor of Kirkcaldy (proprietors of GMC Company q.v.) and put into voluntary liquidation August 1918. Both Chisholm and Jack traded subsequently and separately.

Routes:

Dunfermline – Kelty via Lassodie September 1914-August 1918
Dunfermline – Rosyth via Queensferry Road July 1915-May 1918
Dunfermline – Inverkeithing July 1915-January 1916 and May 1918-August 1918 extended -- Aberdour (Sundays only)
Inverkeithing – Rosyth January 1916-May 1918
Dunfermline – Limekilns February 1917-August 1918

Vehicles:

8.14	?	?	?	?	?	ni
5.15	?	?	?	?	?	ni
6.15	?	?	?	?	?	ni
9.15	?	?	?	?	?	ni
11.15	SP2476	Caledon	?	?	B28	ni
11.15	SP2477	Lothian	?	SMT	B32R	ni
2.16	SP2658	Caledon	?	?	B28	ni
7.16	S 4909	?	?	?	?	ni
7.16	SP2792	?	?	?	?	ni
7.17	SP2651	Caledon	?	?	?	ni
3.18	S 7446	Caledon	?	?	B30	ni
5.18	S 7447	Caledon	?	?	B30	ni

BALD Andrew Bald, Kelty

Operated Ford 'T' from Kelty to Saline for short period only. No further information.

73. *The Autocar Bus Company's only Lothian was SP 2477, photographed when new. While the SMT Co built and operated many Lothians, sales to other operators were limited.*

BAXTER'S (trading as ABC) — Alexander Baxter, 95 High Street, Cowdenbeath

Livery: Originally Yellow, later Light and Dark Blue with Red mid-band

Alex Baxter had a cycle business and purchased his first bus in 1924, running to Kinross then Milnathort. A Saturday service was run to Glen Lomond Sanitorium. The Kinross service was extended to Perth and a Cowdenbeath to Inverkeithing route also was operated. A working agreement was reached with Kelty MT Company and A&A Young in May 1931 but this was shortlived, the business being purchased by Alexander on 16 September 1931.

Vehicles:

1.24	SP4208	Clyde	?	Stewart	B20	'The Raleigh'
oq.24	TS2142	Thornycroft	?	?	B32R	ex Dundee (Corporation?)
oq.?	?	Dennis	?	Normand & Thomson	?	Chassis ex WD
10.24	SP9270	Spa	?	Eaton	B20F	ni
5.25	FG 254	Halley QSX	2971	Normand & Thomson	B26	Body ex Dennis. To GMC (O214)
3.26	FG1332	Albion PJ26	5002L	?	B31	Body ex Thornycroft. To GMC (C211)
3.27	FG2650	Albion PM28	7005C	?	?	To GMC (D62)
5.27	FG3126	Albion PK26	5038I	?	B26	To GMC (C208)
3.28	FG3880	Albion PK26	5058D	?	B26	To GMC (C209)
oq.29	SC1846	Dennis	17518	Croall	B32	ex White Line Edinburgh. To GMC (D208)
oq.29	SC1848	Dennis	17536	Croall	B32	ex White Line Edinburgh. To GMC (D209)
3.29	FG4806	Albion PKA26	5078L	?	C26	To GMC (C210)

BEATTIE'S MOTOR SERVICE — James Beattie, St Margaret's Street, Dunfermline

Established March 1917 as taxi operator, bus run from 1921. No record after licence of two vehicles by Dunfermline Magistrates in April 1925.

Routes:

Dunfermline – Charlestown via Limekilns May 1921
Dunfermline – Aberdour, Sundays only June 1921
Dunfermline – Cowdenbeath (June 1922). May have briefly run to Perth from September 1922.

Vehicles:

5.21	SP5949	AEC	B2857	?	B20	To A. Factor 11.22
7.21	SP6219	Albion	?	?	B34	ni (used town gas)

No information on further vehicles.

BERNARD — James Bernard, Station Road, Dunfermline

Livery: Fawn and Red

Established 1926 and ran in Lochore 'Co-operative' for some time. Bus business including one licence transferred to Turner of Kelty, September 1927. Operated taxi service thereafter.

Routes:

Dunfermline – Cardenden February 1926
Dunfermline – Lochore August 1926 to September 1927

Vehicles:

1.26	FG1127	Morris	?	?	B14	(licence Fife 14)
7.26	FG2028	Morris	?	?	B14	To Turner 9.27; to Dunf. Tramways 10.31

BEVERIDGE — Robert Beveridge, Roscobie by Dunfermline

One vehicle licensed by Dunfermline Magistrates, April 1925. No further details available.

BISSET & GILMOUR — James Bisset (from July 1924) 67 High Street, Burntisland

Chemist and aereated water manufacturer who pioneered the Dunfermline – Burntisland route and later operated it jointly with Simpsons MS and Saline MS. Operations were probably passed to Harrow Scott about July 1924.

Routes:

Dunfermline – Burntisland via Aberdour 5 August 1920 to July 1924

Vehicles:

?	SP2225	Leyland?	?	?	Ly/Ch30	Interchangeable Body
c7.20	SP4789	Thornycroft	?	?	ch 32	ni
5.21	SP5880	Albion	?	?	ch ?	ni
oq 11.21	SP3630	Thornycroft	?	?	ch 30	ni

74. *Outing from Burntisland with Bisset & Gilmour's Thornycroft SP 4789. The urchin on the right seems determined to get into the scene.*

75. *Jim Blyth's Model 'T' Ford charabanc SP 6801, photographed in 1923 on a trip to Rumbling Bridge.*

BLYTH'S MOTOR SERVICE
J. Blyth, Rossend Avenue, Burntisland

Commenced operation Burntisland to Dunfermline April 1922, vehicle purchased from Harry K. Brown of Kirkcaldy (body may have been built by them). Withdrawn, probably after spectacular run-away down Dunfermline's New Row.

Vehicles:

4.22	SP6801	Ford 'T'	?	Brown?	Ly/ch 14	ni

76. *Builder's record photo, taken 19 October 1926 of Brand's brand-new Albion FG 1724 which passed to Forrester's in May 1928.*

BRAND'S MOTOR SERVICE
James Brand, Dunfermline

Livery: Tawny Red

Former partner (with Jas. Chisholm) in Saline Motor Service. Given Forte's times on Dunfermline to Lochore operating group after Fortes accident in September 1926. In May 1928 these times were passed to A & A Young.

Routes:
    Dunfermline – Lochore via Lochgelly September 1926 to May 1928

Vehicle:

8.26	FG1724	Albion PK26	5012L	Jackson	B26D	To Forrester 5.28 (licence F73)

BROWN'S MOTOR SERVICE
James Brown, 81 Perth Road, Cowdenbeath

Livery: Chocolate Brown

Commenced on Dunfermline – Lochore route and became member of operators group. Timings on this service passed to Simpsons Motor Service, November 1928.

Vehicles:

6.24	SP8933	?	?	?	B14	Sold 12.25
12.25	SF3834	?	?	?	B20	ni (licence F10)
aq?	SF3235	Reo	?	?	B24	ni

                                         John Brown, Gordon Street, Cowdenbeath

Livery: Purple

Joined the fray on the Dunfermline to Lochore route in February 1925. Passed vehicle and timings to Andrew Peattie Jnr. in February 1926.

Vehicles:

2.25	SP9649	Chevrolet	?	?	B14	Sold 12.25
12.25	FG1025	Reo	?	?	B20F	To Peattie 2.26 (licence F9)

(repossessed by Fife Motor Co and re-sold to A. Peattie)

CHISHOLM'S MOTOR SERVICE   **John Chisholm, 49 Halbeath Road, Dunfermline**

Chisholm's third, and so far as is known, final bus venture — after the Autocar Bus Co and the Saline MS. In 1927 he was granted permission to operate on the Dunfermline to Burntisland route. After October 1927 some of his runs were taken by Simpsons MS, who may shortly have absorbed all operations.

Vehicles:

aq 3.27	FG 654	Berliet	30677	?	B20	ex Saline MS; Dstd. by fire 10.27
aq 1.28	MS6491	Reo	?	?	B22	ni

COUSIN'S MOTOR SERVICE (C.M.S.)   **Tom and John Cousin, The Garage, Culross**

Livery: Royal Blue

Tom Cousin purchased the long established horse bus business of his employer, Herdman of Culross (with 4 brakes and 1 wagonette) in February 1901 — they had the contract to carry the Royal Mail to Culross. Said to have operated Fife's first motor bus but this seems unlikely given all the existing evidence. His first motor buses were licensed by Dunfermline Town Council in June 1909.
Operated Dunfermline — Culross — Alloa (June 1921) — Kincardine (July 1922), also to High Valleyfield and Blairhall.
Business acquired by the Scottish General Omnibus Co of Falkirk, vesting date 30 May 1925, including those vehicles marked thus * (SGO Co fleet number given where known).

Vehicles:

	6.09	?	Albion	?	?	Ch10	ni
	6.09	SP 620	Halley	?	?	Ch15	ni
3	3.13	SP1089	Commer	?	?	Ch25	'Royal Blue Third'
	7.13	V 1819	Halley	?	?	Ch29	'St Serf'
	.14	V 2367	Halley	?	?	Ch29	'St Mungo'
	6.15	?	Commer?	?	?	Ch20/B28	ni
	2.16	GA1348	Halley	?	?	B28/B45	ni
7	9.16	GA1349	Halley	?	?	B37	'Number Seven'
	12.16	SP2877	Halley	?	?	B32	*(?); to Wemyss 6.29
	6.19	SP3222	Halley	B2.1817	?	B24	Sold 1. 21 to Carmichael
	6.19	SP3455	Halley	?	?	B35F	ni
1	.20	SP4901	Halley	?	?	Ch26	*(83); to Wemyss 6.29
	.21	SG1570	Lothian	?	SMT	B32R	*(?); to Dunfermline Tmys 7.27
	.21	SG2205	AEC	?	?	B32	Sold 12.22 to Carmichael
	.21	SG2320	Leyland	?	?	B32F	Sold .25 to Kelty MT Co
	5.21	SP5167	Star?	?	?	?	Sold 12.23
	5.21	SP5956	Guy	?	Bartol	B20F	Sold 7.24 to Ramsay #
	aq 7.21	SY1330	Dennis	12936	Strachan & Brown	Ch32	*(86); ex SMT; (ex Adam Young)
12	7.21	SP6119	Thornycroft J	6151	SMT	B32	*(80?); to GMC
	10.21	SP6446	Fiat	?	?	B14	*(?); to Dunfermline Tmys 7.27
	.22	SG5716	Lothian	?	SMT	B32R	ni
	6.22	SP7036	Lothian	?	SMT	Ch?	*(85); to GMC 11.26
	2.23	SP7584	Daimler	?	?	B ?F	ni
	aq 9.23	NW3563	Thornycroft X	9733	Strachan & Brown	B35	*(87); to GMC **
	5.24	SP8782	Lancia	?	?	Ch18	*(?); to Dunfermline Tmys 7.27
	5.24	SP8783	Lancia	?	?	Ch18	*(?); to Dunfermline Tmys 7.27?
	5.24	SP8965	Leyland	20191	?	B32	*(91)
	7.24	SP9022	Dennis	?	Strachan & Brown	B25F	*(88)
	8.24	SP9372	Lothian	?	SMT	B32R	*(?); to GMC 1.27
	5.25	FG243	Minerva	?	?	B20	*(84); to Wemyss 6.29

* These vehicles to SGO Co 30.5.25 (nos 79-94)   # This vehicle 1921 Motor Show exhibit   **ex demonstrator new 6.23

OPPOSITE: 77. *Cousins' Halley of (probably) 1909, SP 620 — from a faded old photograph;* **78.** *Commer SP 1089 'Royal Blue Third' with Tom Cousins in charge;*   **79.** *Halley SP 3455 of 1919 photographed in Pittencrieff Street, Dunfermline;* **80.** *John Cousins with 6-cylinder Halley SP 4901 of 1920 (see also fig.43);* **81.** *Daimler SP 7584, was new in February 1923. Note the 'trafficator' — a board with painted hand;* **82.** *Lancia charabanc SP 8782 was 6ft. wide to allow it to tour on the narrow Trossachs roads;* **83.** *Two of Cousins' Lothians, built by SMT in Edinburgh, in front of the Culross garage. Included in the line-up are John Cousins (on L) and John Fotheringham (3 from L). Both vehicles went to SGO Co and then to other operators.*

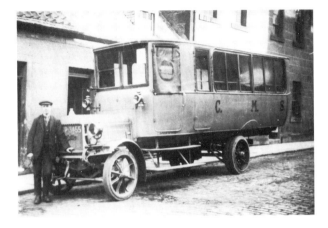

CULLEN

Hugh Cullen, 53 High Street, Dunfermline

One vehicle licenced by Dunfermline Magistrates, May 1924. No details of this vehicle or route operated (if any).

COLQUHOUN

J. Colquhoun, Netherton Street, Dunfermline

Was noted as a bus proprietor running from Dunfermline to Rosyth in June 1912. No information on vehicle or duration of service.

DAVIDSON

John C. Davidson, Black Road, Kelty

Established by 1924 operating Kelty – Kinross – Milnathort and eventually Cowdenbeath to Perth. Business acquired in March 1928 by A & A Young, also of Kelty.

Vehicles:

?	SP1234	Reo	?	?	B	Dstd. by fire 12.30
?	SP9433?	Ford	?	?	B	ni
1.25	SP9738	Lancia	?	?	B20F	To Young 3.28
aq 2.26	VA3903	Lancia	?	Strachan & Brown	B26F	To Young 3.28
?	?	De Dion	?	?	?	ni
?	?	Minerva	?	?	?	ni

84. *Three of Davidson's buses photographed outside his garage in Black Road, Kelty; from the left, SP 9738, SP 9433 (?), VA 3903.*

DIVITO

George Divito, Seaside Place, Aberdour

Livery: Grey

Established about October 1924 operating Dunfermline – Lochgelly – Lochore. (Also traded as George Davie). One licence (F18) which passed to Peattie Brothers of Glencraig in November 1928.

Vehicles:

aq 10.24	SP4273	Fiat 2FO	172276	?	Ch14	ex Saline MS. Sold 4.25
aq 4.25	GB8894	Reo	?	?	B20F	to Peattie Bros. 11.28

DUNFERMLINE MOTOR SERVICE (D.M.S.)

J. Carmichael & Son, 140 Rumblingwell, Dunfermline

Commenced operation in 1921 running miners to Valleyfield, later operated Dunfermline to Saline via Blairhall. Purchased by Alexander, October 1931.

Vehicles:

aq c 1.21	SP3222	Halley	B2.1817	?	ex Cousins MS
aq 2.22	CX2873	?	?	?	Sold 11.25
aq 12.22	SG2205	AEC	?	?	ex Cousins MS
aq 3.25	SP9990	?	?	?	To Dunfermline Tmys 2.28
11.25	FG 948	?	?	?	ni

Other vehicles were owned, as the fleet was quoted as being four buses in April 1925.

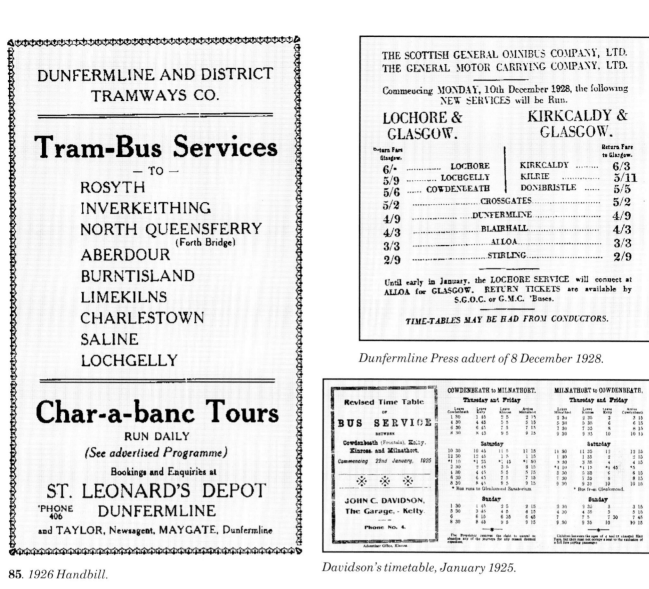

DUNFERMLINE AND DISTRICT TRAMWAYS CO.

Tram-Bus Services

— TO —

ROSYTH
INVERKEITHING
NORTH QUEENSFERRY
(Forth Bridge)
ABERDOUR
BURNTISLAND
LIMEKILNS
CHARLESTOWN
SALINE
LOCHGELLY

Char-a-banc Tours

RUN DAILY

(See advertised Programme)

Bookings and Enquiries at

ST. LEONARD'S DEPOT

'PHONE
406   **DUNFERMLINE**

and TAYLOR, Newsagent, MAYGATE, Dunfermline

85. *1926 Handbill.*

THE SCOTTISH GENERAL OMNIBUS COMPANY, LTD.
THE GENERAL MOTOR CARRYING COMPANY, LTD.

Commencing MONDAY, 10th December 1928, the following
NEW SERVICES will be Run.

LOCHORE & GLASGOW.		KIRKCALDY & GLASGOW.
Return Fare Glasgow.		Return Fare to Glasgow.
6/- .... LOCHORE	KIRKCALDY	6/3
5/9 .... LOCHGELLY	KILRIE	5/11
5/6 ...... COWDENBEATH	DONIBRISTLE	5/5
5/2 .... CROSSGATES		5/2
4/9 .... DUNFERMLINE		4/9
4/3 .... BLAIRHALL............		4/3
3/3 .... ALLOA............		3/3
2/9 .... STIRLING............		2/9

Until early in January, the LOCHORE SERVICE will connect at
ALLOA for GLASGOW. RETURN TICKETS are available by
S.G.O.C. or G.M.C. 'Buses.

TIME-TABLES MAY BE HAD FROM CONDUCTORS.

Dunfermline Press advert of 8 December 1928.

Davidson's timetable, January 1925.

86. *This garage was built in 1924 at St. Leonards, Dunfermline, to house the 'Tram-bus' fleet. Two of their Tilling-Stevens buses are on the left. Behind these, and on the right are 'General' buses – solid tyred, while the others have the newer pneumatic tyres.*

Livery: Dark Red and Cream

Established April 1924 as bus operator, but operated trams from 1909. Bus operations commenced to combat effect of pirate buses on tram routes, then to compete on established routes to obtain control where possible. Close working relationship with Scottish General Omnibus Co (Larbert) as both were part of Fife Tramway Light and Power Company. Bus department of Tramway Company vested in SGO Co in March 1926 and vehicles numbered into SGO Co series. In March 1930 the SGO Co and all its many subsidiaries were purchased in the name of W Alexander & Sons as the chosen nominee by powers granted under the 1929 Railways Act. Operators remained nominally independent for some time, and some acquired vehicles were transferred into ownership of the Tramway Company.

Routes:
  Dunfermline – Inverkeithing commenced 3 April 1924
  Dunfermline – Lochgelly commenced 3 April 1924
  Dunfermline – Burntisland commenced 3 April 1924
  Dunfermline – North Queensferry commenced 3 April 1924
  Dunfermline – Saline by September 1924
  Dunfermline – Charlestown by May 1925

Vehicles:

1	3.24	SP8741	Tilling-Stevens TS3A	3101	?	B26F	
2	3.24	SP8742	Tilling-Stevens TS3A	?	?	B26F	
3	3.24	SP8743	Tilling-Stevens TS3A	?	?	B26F	SGO No 97
4	3.24	SP8744	Tilling-Stevens TS3A	?	?	B26F	SGO No 98
5	3.24	SP8745	Tilling-Stevens TS3A	3104	?	B26F	
7	3.24	SP8759	Tilling-Stevens TS3A	3106	?	B26F	
	3.24	SP8760	Tilling-Stevens TS3A	3099	?	B26F	
	4.24	SP8830	Tilling-Stevens TS3A	?	?	B26F	
	4.24	SP8831	Tilling-Stevens TS3A	3105	?	B26F	SGO No 102
	4.24	SP8868	Tilling-Stevens TS3A	3108	?	B26F	
	6.24	SP9139	Tilling-Stevens TS3A	3124	?	B26F	SGO No 105
	6.24	SP9140	Tilling-Stevens TS3A	3125	?	B26F	SGO No 106
	9.24	SP9426	Tilling-Stevens TS3A	?	?	B26F	
	9.24	SP9427	Tilling-Stevens TS3A	?	?	B26F	
	9.24	SP9428	Tilling-Stevens TS3A	3225	?	B26F	
	9.24	SP9429	Tilling-Stevens TS3A	?	?	B26F	
17	11.24	SP9550	Albion PE24	4031D	?	B20F	
18	11.24	SP9551	Albion PE24	4032E	?	B20F	
19	11.24	SP9552	Albion PE24	4046H	?	B20F	
20	11.24	SP9553	Albion PE24	4046I	?	B20F	
	3.25	SP9920	Albion PE24	4072B	?	B20F	
	3.25	SP9921	Albion PE24	4073D	?	B20F	
	3.25	SP9922	Albion PE24	4073E	?	B20F	
	3.25	SP9923	Albion PE24	4074E	?	B20F	
25	5.25	FG 246	Albion PH24	4074D	?	Ch19	
	5.25	FG 247	Albion PH24	4075E	?	Ch19	
	5.25	FG 281	Tilling-Stevens T53A	3251	?	Ch29	SGO No 121
	5.25	FG 282	Tilling-Stevens T53A	3252	?	Ch29	
	aq 7.27	SP6446	Fiat	?	?	B14	ex Cousins via SGO Co
	aq 7.27	SP8782	Lancia	?	?	Ch18	ex Cousins via SGO Co
	aq 7.27	SG1570	Lothian	?	SMT	B32R	ex Cousins via SGO Co
	2.28	FG3752	Albion	5048B	?	B28	to W Alexander 12.31
	aq 2.28	FG1767	?	?	?	?	ex Hunter sold 3.31
	aq 2.28	FG3279	?	?	?	?	ex Hunter sold 9.31
	aq 2.28	SP8965	Leyland	?	?	?	ex Ramsay to Alexander 1930
	aq 2.28	FG3143	Guy	?	?	?	ex Ramsay
	aq 2.28	SP9990	?	?	?	?	ex Carmichael sold 6.28
	aq 3.28	FG1857	Dodge	?	?	B20	ex Saline MS sold 8.30
	aq 4.28	FG3175	Guy	?	?	B26	ex Knox Scr 2.33
	aq 10.31	FG2028	Morris	?	?	B14	ex Turner to Alexander 12.31
	aq 10.31	FG4294	Albion	?	?	B26F	ex Turner to Alexander 12.31
	aq 11.31	FG4170	Karrier	?	?	?	ex Scott to Alexander 12.31
	aq 11.31	FG4366	Karrier	?	?	?	ex Scott to Alexander 12.31
	aq 11.31	HS5112	Albion	?	?	?	ex ??

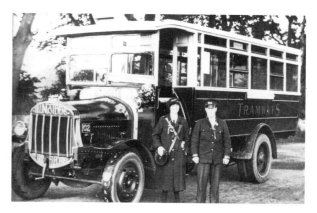

87. *Fine study of Tilling-Stevens number 7 of the Dunfermline Tramways bus fleet. SP 8759.*

88. *After integration with the SGO fleet the livery changed, as did the fleet numbers. 102 (SP 8831) now has pneumatic tyres (with a 'gaiter' on the nearside one).*

89. *The 20-seat Albions were much faster than the Tilling-Stevens buses and took over many of the regular services. SP 9552 was photographed in Charlestown with driver Jack Ramsay and conductress Peggy Lyall.*

90. *Albion charabanc No 25, FG 246, photographed outside the Dunfermline garage in 1925. The building is still in use today by Fife Scottish Buses.*

| FACTOR | | | | | | | Augustus (Gusty) Factor, 24 Jigburn Terrace, Castleblair |

Commenced operations from Dunfermline to Steelend in February 1921, then to Saline from November 1922. Last licence issued May 1924.

Vehicles:

?	?	?		?	?	?	
2.22	SP5228	?		?	?	10	sold 3.22 to W Smith
3.22	SP6356	?		?	?	14	ni
aq 11.22	SP5949	AEC'B'		?	?	B20	ex Beattie
1.24	SP5770	?		?	?	6	Sold 3.24
aq 3.24	S 5176	Palladium		?	?	14	ni

Stated to have owned a Daimler and a Reo.

| F.M.T. | | | | | Fife Motor Transit Co Ltd, Hunter Street, Kirkcaldy |

Founded in February 1909 – Fife's first motor bus operator. Great ambitions initially to operate motor buses throughout West Fife. Financial support was not forthcoming, but not a great deal of time was allowed for the operation to establish itself. Perhaps the prospect of the imminent opening of tramways was considered reason to abandon the short-lived service. Operation from Cowdenbeath to Lochgelly commenced on 2 February 1909 and ceased on 4 March, just one month later.

Vehicle:

2.09	?	Arrol-Johnson	?	?	B36	returned to makers 3.09

| FORTE | | | | | Antonio Forte, 81 Main Street, Lochgelly |

Commenced running March 1926 on the Dunfermline – Lochore route and given times on the combined timetable. Licence withdrawn after fatal accident when the bus collided with a tramcar in September 1926. The licence was ultimately transferred to Simpson's Motor Service, November 1928.

Vehicle:

3.26	FG1383	Reo	?	?	B24	to Simpsons MS 11.28

91. *John Fotheringham's second bus was this neat 20-seat Reo Speed Wagon, bodied by Metcalfe. He later gave up operation and became a driver for Alexander.*

'CULROSS MOTOR SERVICE' — John Fotheringham, Orchard View, Culross

Livery: Dark Red

Former driver of Cousins MS who, after Cousins purchased by SGO Co, attempted to compete with them on the Culross and later High Valleyfield route.

Vehicles:

2.26	FG1235	Reo		?	?	B20	sold 2.29
?	GD1616	Reo		?	Metcalfe	B20F	ni
2.29	TS7731	Albion PKA26	5073H		Dickson	B26	registered by Dickson in Dundee 1.29

FROGGAT — William Froggat, Dunfermline

From January 1929, ran Dunfermline to Inverkeithing, but by February was running to Blairhall and Oakley. It is not known how long this continued.

Vehicle:

aq 1.24	EE1400	?		?	?	B14	ni

GOLD LINE — David Gold, Cowdenbeath

Livery: Gold

Operated Cowdenbeath to Dunfermline in winter and to Aberdour on Summer Saturdays. Believed to have given up business after accident in December 1923.

Vehicle:

5.22	SP6925	Ford 'T'		?	?	ch14	'The Earl Haig'

92. *One of Forrester's first Albions, SP 5312 dated from February 1921, photographed at the Company's Lochgelly premises.*

93. *Among Forrester's early vehicles was this Scottish built Clyde, SP 7253. It was built in Wishaw, but did not survive until the 1929 amalgamation.*

Livery: Crimson Red and Cream

Originally ran Transport Department of Lochgelly Coal and Iron Co, then put charabone bodies on lorries to run tours, private hires etc. First service Lochgelly to Kirkcaldy. Business of Stewart of Kirkcaldy (Kirkcaldy to Kinglassie) acquired April 1927. Amalgamated from 1st October 1929 with Simpsons Motor Service, Dunfermline to form Simpson's & Forrester's which operated as the West Fife department of W Alexander as a nominally separate entity until 1938.

Routes:

     Lochgelly – Kirkcaldy – prior to June 1927

     Kinross – Kirkcaldy via Lochore by April 1928

     Lochgelly – Cupar (December 1928) extended to St Andrews from 19 May 1929

     Lochgelly – Newport (for Dundee) from 19 May 1929

     Kirkcaldy – Perth via Auchtermuchty

Vehicles:

	9.19	?	Albion	?	?	Ch/lry	ex W.D. chassis	
	5.20	SP4207	Leyland	?	?	Ch	ni	
	.20	SP4551	?	?	?	?	ni	
	.20	SP4589	Clyde	?	?	B?	Sold 9.22	
	2.21	SP5312	Albion	?	?	Ch	ni	
	7.22	SP7253	Clyde	44	?	Ch	ni	
28?	6.25	FG 576	Leyland C9	?	?	26	*	
30?	6.25	FG 577	Leyland C9	?	?	26	*	
34	3.26	FG1341	Leyland	35938	?	B28	*	
29	5.26	FG1763	Leyland C9	36304	?	Ch29	*dstd. by fire 9.32	
33	5.26	FG1764	Leyland C9	36303	?	Ch28	*	
35	5.27	FG3028	Leyland C9	36831	?	C29F	*dstd. by fire 9.32	
36	aq 5.27	MS7129	Albion PJ24	4207C	Alexander	B24F	*rgd by Alexander 3.27 dstd. by fire 9.32	
37	aq 5.27	MS7130	Albion PJ24	4201F	Alexander	B24F	*rgd by Alexander 3.27	
38	aq 7.27	MS7458	Albion PK26	5038J	Alexander	B29F	*rgd by Alexander 5.27 dstd. by fire 9.32	
39?	aq .27	GM 704	Karrier	?	?	B20	*ex Stewart, Kirkcaldy, 4.27	
40	aq 3.28	MS 7653	Leyland PLSC3	45876	Alexander	B32F	*rgd by Alexander 8.27	
41	aq 5.28	FG1724	Albion PK26	5012L	Jackson	B26R	*ex Brand, new 8.26	
42	aq .28	ES6649	Lancia	320	Crerar	Ch20	*ex Stark, Baillieston (?) new 1925	
43	aq 7.28	MS7857	Albion PK26	5053K	Alexander	B26F	*regd by Alexander 5.28	
44	aq 7.28	MS7858	Albion PK26	5053B	Alexander	B26F	*rgd by Alexander 5.28	
45	6.28	FG4166	Albion PK26	5064B	?	B29F	*	
46	9.28	FG4417	Leyland PLSC	47455	Alexander	B35F	*	
47	4.29	FG4929	Leyland TS1	60248	Alexander	B32	*	
48	4.29	FG4930	Leyland TS1	60252	Alexander	B32	*	
49	5.29	FG4996	Leyland TS1	60272	Alexander	B32	*	
50	5.29	FG4997	Leyland TS1	60277	Alexander	B32	*	
51	7.29	FG5334	Leyland TD1	70781	Leyland	L24/24R	*	
52	7.29	FG5335	Leyland TD1	70782	Leyland	L24/24R	*	
53	7.29	FG5267	Albion PKA26	5087D	?	B29F	*	
54	7.29	FG5271	Albion PMA28	7054L	?	B32	*	
55	7.29	FG5272	Albion PMA28	7055B	?	B32	*	
56	7.29	FG5300	Albion PKA26	5088A	?	B28F	*	
32	8.29	FG5378	Leyland LT1	50514	Leyland	B35F	*	

* These vehicles to Simpson's and Forrester's 1.10.29 (numbered only after amalgamation).

94. *Three of Forrester's buses in Cowdenbeath, FG 4166, nearest the camera, is a 1928 Albion which became number 45 in the combined fleet.*

HARRISON
Thomas Harrison, Kingseat

Operating Kingseat — Dunfermline in October 1921. Still operating 1922 but not established when operation ceased.

Vehicle:

10.21	SP6316	?	?	?	B14	

Two vehicles owned in May 1922

HENDRY
Charles Hendry, Tullohill, Saline

Commenced operation December 1921, Dunfermline to Saline, extended to Blairhall by October 1924, and to Dollar in June 1927.

Vehicles:

12.21	SP6498	?	?	?	14	ni
?	?	Commer	?	?	Ch20	ni
aq 1.24	SG8612	?	?	?	14	ni
aq 5.24	SP3921	?	?	?	14	ni
10.25	FG 913	Beardmore	?	?	14	to Ramsay (Lassodie MS) 3.27
aq 6.27	GM 795	Beardmore	?	?	14	ni

HUNTER'S
Thomas and Cathcart Hunter, Hollybush, Newmills

Former Cousins employee who operated route from Dunfermline to Culross from July 1925 after Cousins operations taken over by SGO Co, later ran Dunfermline to Kincardine. Acquired by SGO Co in February 1928, vehicles in to Dunfermline Tramways fleet.

Vehicles:

7.25	FG 603	Ford	?	?	B14	ni
5.26	FG1767	?	?	?	?	To Dunfermline Tmys 2.28
7.27	FG3279	?	?	?	?	To Dunfermline Tmys 2.28

JACK
George Jack, Bellyeoman Road, Dunfermline

Operated from Dunfermline to Aberdour from July 1921, probably passed to Wests in 1924.

Vehicle:

7.21	SP5677	Karrier	2905	Jackson	B30	To Wests c24

KELTY MOTOR TRANSPORT COY
Wm Milne & Wm McLean, Oakfield Street, Kelty

Livery: Dark Green

Established 1920, formed combine with A & A Young and Baxter May 1931 then purchased by Alexander in September 1931.

Routes:

Dunfermline — Kelty via Lassodie (November 1921)
Cowdenbeath — Milnathort from 22 June 1922 later extended to Perth
Dunfermline — Cupar from 13 May 1929 extended to St Andrews via Dairsie and Guardbridge from 29 July 1929

Vehicles:

	c5.20	?	Maudslay ?	?	?	Ch30	ni
	6.22	SP7042	Fiat ?	?	?	?	Sold 3.27
	6.23	SP7984	Leyland	?	?	B30	Sold 3.28
	4.24	SP8827	Leyland	?	?	B29	ni
	1.25	SP9702	Leyland C9	35214	?	B25	ni
	aq 5.25	SG2320	Leyland	?	?	B32	ex Cousins MS
	9.25	FG 840	?	?	?	?	Sold 11.26
	11.25	FG 991	Reo	1540	?	B20	Sold 11.28
1	8.26	FG2214	Leyland PLSC1	45106	Leyland	B31	To Alexander (L71)
2	5.27	FG3039	Leyland PLSC1	45777	?	B31F	To Alexander (L72)
3	9.27	FG3383	Leyland PLSC3	46120	Leyland	B36F	To Alexander (L73)
4	4.28	FG3940	Leyland PLSC3	46729	?	B32	To Alexander (L74)
5	11.28	FG4475	Leyland PLSC3	47560	Leyland	B F	To Alexander (L75)
6	4.29	FG4995	Albion PKA26	5080A	?	B29	ni
7	6.29	FG5106	Leyland LT1	50170	Alexander	B32F	To Alexander (N128)
8	6.29	FG5207	Leyland LT1	50171	Jackson	C32F	To Alexander (N129)
9	7.29	FG5208	Albion PKA26	5087K	?	B30R	ni
10	8.29	FG5327	Leyland TS1	60351	Leyland	B31F	To Alexander (P102)
11	8.29	FG5377	AEC Reliance	660384	Jackson	B30F	To Alexander (0204)
12	1.30	FG5698	Leyland TS1	60728	?	B32F	To Alexander (P103)
13?	aq 2.30	OU3135	Thornycroft	?	?	B32	ni
14	3.30	FG5798	Leyland TS1	60981	?	B32F	To Alexander (P104)
16	5.30	FG6082	Leyland TS2	60701	?	B30	To Alexander (P106)
15	7.30	FG6269	Leyland TS3	61231	Leyland	B32F	To Alexander (P105)
17	4.31	FG6838	Leyland TS1	61417	Jackson?	?	To Alexander (P107)

KNOX

Operated from Dunfermline to Alloa via Culross, commencing in June 1927. Business purchased by SGO Co in February 1928. Knox recommenced operations in Wick, operating the 'Pioneer' service to Thurso.

Vehicles:

6.27	FG3175	Guy	?	?	B24	to Dunfermline Tmys 4.28
by 9.27	GD754	?	?	?	B14	ni

LASSODIE MOTOR SERVICE

Established by September 1923, working from Philp's yard in Dunfermline. Gave up original Lassodie run after severe competition from Kelty Motor Transport Co. Concentrated thereafter on Dunfermline to Saline via Redcraigs.

Vehicles:

by 9.23	?	?	?	?	?	ni
aq 7.24	SP5956	Guy	?	Bartol	B20	ex Cousins MS
9.25	FG 863	Karrier	?	?	B26	ni
4.26	FG1546	Chevrolet	?	?	B14	ni
aq 3.27	FG 913	Beardmore	?	?	B14	ex Hendry
6.27	FG3143	Guy	?	?	B26	to Dunfermline Tmys 2.28

95. *Kelty MY Co No 2, Leyland FG 3039, seen in Kinross en route to Cowdenbeath.*

96. *Rear end of KMT Leyland No 8, FG 5207, which had a partly removable roof.*

97. *Kelty MT Co bought some bodies from Jackson's, Bodybuilders of Dunfermline. This included their only AEC vehicle, number 11, FG 5377, seen here in Jackson's yard.*

McEWAN

Horse bus proprietor of long-standing purchased his first motor bus in December 1914. His licence was last renewed on 26 April 1920, two vehicles being then owned.

Vehicle:

12.14	?	?	?	?	ch28	ni

MILLER'S MOTOR SERVICE
Dougald Miller, The Mansions, Cairneyhill

Livery: Red with Tartan band on waist

Former driver with Cousins of Culross, established his own operations from Dunfermline to Culross in July 1926. Purchased by SGO Co c June 1928 but separate identity and fleetname used until after April 1930.

Routes:

Dunfermline — Culross via Cairneyhill from July 1926
Dunfermline — Steelend from July 1926
Dunfermline — Stirling via Kincardine (joint with SGO Co) from April 1927
Culross — Alloa via Kincardine from 6 April 1930

Vehicles:

7.26	FG2012	Albion	5012B	Jackson	B26F	SGO Co (189) Alexander (C160)
12.26	FG2402	Albion PM28	7001I	Jackson	B32F	SGO Co (190) Alexander (D44)
3.27	FG2774	Albion	5021G	Jackson	B26F	SGO Co (191) Alexander (C113)
7.27	FG3284	Albion	5041E	Jackson	B26F	SGO Co (192) Alexander (C161)
12.27	FG3611	Albion	5044J	Jackson	B26F	SGO Co (193) Alexander (C34)
11.28	FG4552	Dennis	70337	?	B14	Dst by fire 3.30
6.29	FG5168	Dennis	70523	?	B?	ni
11.29	FG5519	Dodge	?	?	B20	ni

98. *Dougald Miller's Albion FG 2774 was photographed in Cairneyhill Main Street. It later served with Alexander, re-bodied, on the Kirkcaldy tram replacement service.*

MITCHELL
J Mitchell Jnr, Station Road, Kelty

Livery: Bright Green

Established by March 1925 operating Dunfermline to Lochgelly, extended to cover from route to Lochore after November 1925. New route from Dunfermline to Kirkcaldy via Kilrie commenced from 7 November 1927. Business acquired by SGO Co in October 1931.

Vehicles:

3.25	SP9863	Reo	?	?	B14F	Licence F11
7.25	FG 624	Reo	?	?	B26F	Licence F12
2.26	SF3988	Reo	?	?	B14	Licence F13
?	SN3510	?	?	?	?	ni
?	GD4489	Halley?	?	?	?	ni
7.27	SX2145	Reo	?	?	B20R	ni
6.30	SL1372	?	?	?	?	ni

PEATTIE
Andrew Peattie Jnr, 74 New Cottages, Lochore

Livery: Purple

Commenced operations on Dunfermline to Lochore via Lochgelly run in September 1925. Operated separately from D & J Peattie, then joined forces in 1928. Taken over by Alexander c September 1931. * these two to Peattie Bros.

Vehicles:

9.25	FG 598	Morris	?	?	B14	Licence F20
3.26	FG1236	Reo	?	?	B20F	* Dst by fire 3.31
aq 2.26	FG1025	Reo	?	?	B20F	* ex Brown Cbth, to Alexander (O194)

99. *Reo FG 1025 had a varied career. Purchased new by John Brown, Cowdenbeath, it was later with Andrew Pettie, went to Pettie Brothers and ended up with Alexanders.*

PEATTIE BROTHERS

D & J Peattie, Crosshill, Glencraig

Separate operations from Andrew Peattie, working from at least 1927, operating Lochgelly to Kirkcaldy via Kinglassie and Thornton. Joined forces in 1928, taken over by Alexander as noted above.

Vehicles:

aq .27	GD3841	Gilford	?	?	B24	Licence F449
4.27	FG2849	Gilford	?	Dick	B26	Licence F450, to Alexander (Y31)
aq 11.28	GB8894	Reo	?	?	B20F	ex Divito, Licence F451
5.28	FG4113	Albion	5064G	?	B29F	Licence F452, to GMC, to Wemyss Tmys

(When with Peattie Brothers, FG1025 and FG1236 were given Licences F447 and F448 respectively.)

PENROSE

James S Penrose, 64 Church Street, Cowdenbeath

Commenced operation April 1922, Dunfermline to Cowdenbeath, extended soon to Lochore. Also ran Dunfermline to Kelty. Licence to Simpson's MS November 1928.

Vehicles:

12.23	SP8427	Fiat	89092	?	B20	
5.25	FG 53	Reo	?	?	B14	Licence F19

100. *Philp's second acquisition was this Commer, ST 256, purchased secondhand in 1912.*

PHILP'S BUS SERVICE

William Philp, St Margaret's Street, Dunfermline

Horse bus proprietor running Dunfermline to Lochgelly then expanding by the purchases of other operators, to Kelty, to Saline (Keirs purchased 1903) and Steelend. Lochgelly and Kelty abandoned on opening of tramway. Motor bus operation commenced in September 1911 running from Dunfermline to Charlestown via Limekilns. Route to Saline also operated. Operation may have been purchased by West Fifeshire Motor Bus Service Co Ltd in 1917.

Vehicles:

9.11	SP 891	Straker-Squire	?	?	ch28	ni
aq 6.12	ST 256	Commer	?	?	ch28	ex Glenurquhart Motor Car Co
8.12	V 1597	Commer	?	?	ch20	ni
4.14	SP1154	Commer WPI	1040	Kinross	ch35	requisitioned by WD 8.14
3.16	?	Straker-Squire	?	?	ch30	ni

QUEENSFERRY MOTOR CO

One 14-seat bus licenced October 1913. No other reference discovered.

R A MOTOR SERVICE   John Reid, Upper Station Road, Dunfermline

Established January 1923, operating Dunfermline – Blairhall – Oakley from 3 February 1923, later at one stage running Dunfermline to Cowdenbeath.

Vehicle:

aq 1.23	SP6481	Ford		?	?	14	ni

ROBINSON'S   William H Robinson, 19 Kirkgate, Dunfermline

Livery: Maroon

Commenced operating July 1921, Dunfermline to Aberdour then Dunfermline to Limekilns and Charlestown. Business acquired by Simpson's MS, November 1926.

Vehicles:

7.21	SP5223	Ford 'T'		?	?	B14	ni
7.21	SP6192	Albion		?	?	B20	ni
7.24	SP9167	Leyland		?	?	B26	to Simpson's 11.26

ROSYTH MOTORS   Charles Weir and Robert Penman, 35 Castle Crescent, Rosyth

Commenced operation June 1922, running Dunfermline to Inverkeithing, or Aberdour, or Rosyth. Last licence granted May 1924. No further details.

Vehicles:

7.20	SP4310	?		?	?	B32	ni
10.21	SP6499	?		?	?	14	ni
4.22	?	Albion A20	3014J	?		ch	ni

SALINE MOTOR SERVICE   John Chisholm and James Brand, 109 Mill Street, Dunfermline

Livery: Grey (some Yellow)

Founded by John Chisholm in March 1919 after takeover of his Autocar Bus Co (and after withdrawal of West Fife Motor Co from Saline route) which had operated similar routes. Kelty route stopped c April 1921 following loss of trade during miners' strike; Saline abandoned in 1925 following fierce competition from Dunfermline Tramways 'Tram-Bus' service. Further competition from the 'Tram-Bus' on the Aberdour and Burntisland route forced the company into liquidation in January 1926. Operation as a going concern was maintained until March 1928 by Wm Jackson (bus body builder, also of Mill Street) towards his claim against the liquidator. He then disposed of the assets to the Scottish General Omnibus Co. The Saline MS had, for a few months in 1919, operated as 'Chisholms Motor Service', and this name was revived for Chisholms third venture.

Vehicles:

3.19	V1818	Halley?		?	?	ch30	B30 from 7.20
6.19	SP3220	Karrier WDS	2727		Jackson?	ch34	To West c 5.24
9.19	SP3582	Karrier WDS	2894		?	ch36	ni
6.20	SP4272	Karrier WDS	RB1069		?	ch26	ni
6.20	SP4273	Fiat 2FO	172276		?	ch14	To Divito 10.24
3.21	SP5856	Karrier WBS	1916		?	B38	ni
6.21	SP6070	Karrier (?)		?	?	?	Sold 11.26
6.21	SP6521	?		?	?	?	Scrapped 11.27
1.23	ES2462	?		?	Crerar?	?	ni
2.24	SP8425	?		?	?	?	To Brook & Amos, Galashiels 7.25
7.24	SP9240	?		?	Jackson?	B26	ni
7.24	SP9241	AEC		?	?	ch24	Dst by fire 11.27
7.24	SP9242	AEC	202Q47		?	ch24	ni
7.25	FG 654	Berliet	30677		?	B24	To Chisholm MS 3.27
6.26	FG1857	Dodge		?	?	B20	To Dunfermline Tmys 3.28
5.27	GM 761	Lancia		?	?	26	ni
aq 6.28	FG3645	Commer 4GN	6539		?	B30	ex GMC (to replace SP9241)

101. *Saline Motor Services 24-seat AEC charabanc, photographed at Dunfermline's Abbey Gates. The bus was destroyed by fire in November 1927 – a fate which very nearly overtook this old photo many years later. It was – literally – plucked from the flames! Driver Robert Birrell, conductress Liz Beattie.*

SCOTT

Livery: Maroon

Horse bus proprietor, competitor of Cousin on Culross route. Purchased first motor bus in June 1909 (licenced at some sitting of Dunfermline Magistrates as Cousins). Operated Dunfermline to Limekilns and Culross, then Dunfermline to Inverkeithing from November 1921. Business sold up 1922.

Vehicles:

6.09	XS168	Arrol-Johnston	?	?	ch12	ni
5.12	?	Commer	?	?	ly/ch24	ni
9.15	V1366	Halley	?	?	ch35	ni
4.20	SP627_	Daimler	?	?	B28	ni

HARROW SCOTT

Commenced operation July 1924, possibly acquiring business or goodwill of Bisset & Gilmour. Scott's business sold to J. W. Stewart of Rose Street, Kirkcaldy, July 1925. Operated Dunfermline to Burntisland.

Vehicle:

7.24	SP9283	Reo	?	?	B14F	to Stewart, Kirkcaldy 7.25

SCOTT'S BUS SERVICE

Livery: Blue and Cream, later Tawny Red and Cream

Commenced operating from Dunfermline to Lochgelly in February 1924, extended the following year to Lochore. Dunfermline to Culross via Cairneyhill run for a short time from November 1925. Dunfermline to Leven via Lochgelly and Windygates followed, then Dunfermline to Leven via Thornton from July 1929. Purchased by bus combine for Alexanders October 1931, vehicles into Alexanders fleet 1932. During summer months two buses were transferred west and were kept in Munn's garage, Rutherglen, operating on the highly profitable and unregulated Glasgow to Loch Lomond route.

Vehicles:

4.23	SP7751	Guy	94321	?	B14	Sold 8.25
2.24	SP8533	?	?	?	B20	ni (licence F15)
10.24	SP9513	Reo	105296	?	B14	ni (licence F16)
7.25	FG 627	Karrier	10262	Dick	B20	ni (licence F17) sold 6.30
5.26	FG1639	Reo	W2081	?	B26	To Alexander
10.27	GB9854	Reo	?	?	B20	ni
12.27	GM1136	Karrier	?	Stewart	B26	ni (probably destroyed by fire)
6.28	FG4170	Karrier	?	?	?	To Alexander (O135)
8.28	FG4366	Karrier	?	?	?	To Alexander (O136)
5.29	FG5034	Albion PKA26	5079A	?	B29F	To Alexander (C171)
6.30	FG6178	Albion PMA28	7065I	?	B30F	To Alexander (D14)
aq 6.31	DC8778	Albion PR28	7044J	?	B30F	To Alexander (E10) ex Blue Band, Middlesborough

SCOTT'S MOTOR SERVICE

Former Cousins driver who purchased a bus in 1925 to operate Burntisland to Cowdenbeath. After a backfire it burned out in February. Faced with this the undertaking was not resumed.

Vehicle:

aq c 1.25	?	?	?	?	ch14	Burnt out 'nearly new'

102. *Albion FG 6178, owned by Robert Scott and photographed at Lochore Terminus in the short period between its purchase in June 1930 and being acquired by Alexander in October 1931.*

103. *Leyland SP 7900 in St Catherine's Wynd, Dunfermline with Frank Simpson on the left. From here it ran to Inverkeithing and Aberdour. The vehicle looked totally different when it was later fitted with pneumatic tyres.*

104. *Simpson's first Albion was this Valkerie FG 3828, fleet number 13. The official Albion photograph is a fine record of this impressive and stylish vehicle.*

A & J SHARP

A & J Sharp, address not known

Dunfermline Magistrates granted a licence in January 1923 to operate from St Catherine's Wynd to Charlestown. No further licence applications were made and no other reference has been located.

Vehicle:

aq c1.23   S 1102   ?   ?   ?   ?   ni

SIMPSON'S MOTOR SERVICE

Frank and Alex Simpson, Market Street, Dunfermline

Frank Simpson started his career in the motor bus industry as a driver employed by Tom Cousin, later working for David West and Saline MS before purchasing his first bus in early 1923. With this the first service commenced on 8 March, Dunfermline to Inverkeithing, extended from 4 June to Aberdour. By the spring of 1924 operating Dunfermline to Burntisland, jointly then with Saline MS and Bisset & Gilmour. Continued expansions saw new routes to Charlestown, then the Dunfermline to Kirkcaldy run was extended – from May 1929 – to become Stirling to Kirkcaldy via Dunfermline. This was very soon extended, by joint operation with the Scottish General Co of Larbert and GMC of Kirkcaldy to become a major cross-Scotland service linking Glasgow, through Stirling, Dunfermline and Kirkcaldy to Leven or Markinch. Another long service was created when the Dunfermline to Lochgelly run was extended, first to Kinross then to Perth. To compete on an improved basis an understanding was reached with the Lochgelly bus operators A & R Forrester, the amalgamation taking effect from 1 October 1929. Simpson's contributed twenty-seven vehicles, Forrester's twenty-nine. The new Simpson's & Forrester's was closely associated with Walter Alexander and was used as the West Fife operator of the Scottish bus group. The General Motor Conveying Co of Kirkcaldy formed the equivalent east Fife operator; then two operating fleets retaining a nominal independence until 1938.   * these vehicles to Simpson's & Forrester's 1.10.29

Vehicles:

	3.23	SP7471	Fiat	?	?	Bl4	ni
1	5.23	SP7900	Leyland	?	?	B20F	ni
2	6.24	SP9048	Leyland	?	Stewart	ch29	ni
3	6.25	FG 489	Leyland	35470	?	20	*
4	4.26	FG1485	Leyland A13	35838	?	24	*
5	6.26	FG1796	Leyland C7	35940	?	29	*
6	6.26	FG1797	Leyland C7	35941	?	29	*
7	6.26	FG1813	Dodge A	485876	?	20	*
8	aq 11.26	SP9167	Leyland	?	?	B26	ex Robinson, Dunfermline, new 7.24
9	4.27	FG2894	Leyland PLSC1	45749	Leyland	B31F	*
10	5.27	FG2895	Leyland PLSC1	45523	Leyland	B31F	*
12	6.27	FG3210	Dodge A	?	?	ch19	*
11	6.27	FG3211	Leyland PLSC1	45880	Leyland	C29	*
2	11.27	FG3524	Leyland PLSC3	46385	Leyland	B32F	*
?	aq 1.28	SP7749	?	?	?	?	* ex Ramsay, Leslie, new 4.23 Sold 7.30
13	3.28	FG3828	Albion PNA26	5055H	Alexander	B26F	*
14	5.28	FG3951	Leyland PLSC3	46828	Alexander	B32F	*
15	5.28	FG4114	Leyland PLC1	47122	Alexander	B29	*
16	6.28	FG4115	Leyland PLC1	47123	Alexander	B29	*
17?	aq 11.28	FG1383	Reo	?	?	B24	*10.29 ex Forte, new 3.26
1	12.28	FG4561	Leyland TS1	60095	Alexander	C29F	*
8	4.29	FG4949	Leyland TS1	60269	Alexander	B32F	*
18	4.29	FG4950	Leyland TS1	60249	Alexander	B32F	*
19	5.29	FG5001	Leyland TS1	60273	Alexander	C32F	*
20	5.29	FG5002	Leyland TS1	60275	Alexander	B32F	*
21	5.29	FG5059	Leyland TS1	60276	Alexander	B32F	*
22	5.29	FG5060	Leyland TS1	60278	Alexander	B32F	*
23	7.29	FG5252	Leyland TS2	60587	Alexander	B32F	*
24	7.29	FG5264	Albion PKA26	5080I	?	B26	*
25	7.29	FG5291	Albion PKA26	5087J	?	B32	*
26	7.29	FG5292	Albion PMA28	7055L	?	B32	*
27	7.29	FG5293	Albion PMA28	7056F	?	B32	*

105. *Alexander-bodied Leyland No 14 in Simpson's fleet was FG 3951, photographed at Abbey Gates, Dunfermline, in service on the route to Inverkeithing.*

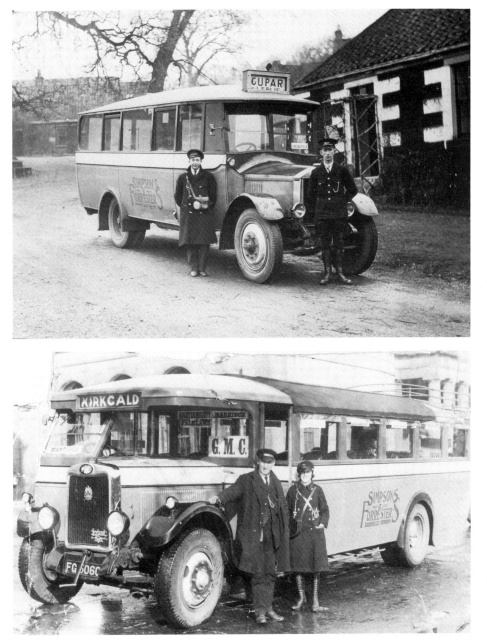

106. *Twenty-four seat Albion MS 7129 was photographed in the picturesque surroundings of Letham village. Number 36 of the combined fleet, it lasted only until September 1932 when it was destroyed in a garage fire.*

107. *Tay Street, Perth was where Leyland FG 5060 was photographed, before setting off for Kirkcaldy. The confused state of affairs is shown when the S & F bus has GMC lettering on the window!*

SIMPSON'S AND FORRESTER'S

Livery: Red, then 'Alexander' Blue

Formed 1 October 1929 to acquire businesses of Simpson's MS, Dunfermline and A & R Forrester's of Lochgelly. Formed West Fife operating area of W Alexander after purchase by Alexander acting on behalf of the powers of the Railways Act. Large degree of integration of vehicles with Alexander and large purchases made of standard types of vehicles. Vehicles purchased after 1931-2 are detailed in other publications, beyond scope of this record.

Vehicles:

1-27	10.29	all ex Simpson's MS Dunfermline qv				
28-56	10.29	all ex A & R Forrester, Lochgelly qv				
57	5.30	FG6042 Leyland LT2	51149	Jackson	B32R	
58-62	aq 6.30	all ex Central Garage, Cupar qv				
63?	aq 2.30	MS6855 Dennis	56706	?	B14F	ex W Alexander (new 8.26)
?	aq 7.30	MS1787 Albion PMA28	7061E	?	C30F	ex GMC

SKED   Thomas Sked

One licence granted by Dunfermline Magistrates in August 1921 for operation from Dunfermline to Steelend. No other reference.

Vehicle:

c 8.21	SP2206 ?		?	?	7	ni

SMITH
William Smith, Mungall Street, Lumphinans

One licence granted by Dunfermline Magistrates in March 1922 for operation from Dunfermline to Culross, then in May 1923 for operation from Dunfermline (Pittencrieff Street) to Valleyfield. No further mentions.

Vehicle:

aq 3.22	SP5228	?	?	?	10	ex A Factor

STOCKS
John S Stocks, Kincardine-on-Forth

Established by end of 1918 operating weekend service from Kincardine to Alloa. Discontinued in 'twenties.

Vehicles:

?	?	Vulcan	?	?	ch/ly	ni
?	?	Thornycroft	?	?	ch/ly	ni

TURNBULL'S MOTOR SERVICE
J Turnbull and W Sneddon, 74 James Street, Dunfermline

One of the earliest post-war operators, running from Dunfermline (Union Inn) to Cowdenbeath (Fountain) from October 1921 until November 1922 when the business was acquired by A & A Young of Kelty.

Vehicle:

aq 10.21	?	Ford 'T'	?	?	ch14	to Young 11.22

TURNER'S MOTOR SERVICE
John Turner, Coronation Place, Kelty

Livery: Chev., Navy Blue; Morris, Russet; 1st Albion, Light Green; 2nd Albion, Dark Green

Operated initially from Lochgelly to Dunfermline, from June 1924. In September 1927 acquired business of Jas Bernard and then concentrated on Dunfermline to Lochore via Lochgelly. Purchased by Alexander October 1931, vehicles into Alexander fleet 1932.

Vehicles:

6.24	SP9060	Chevrolet	?	?	ch14	ni
aq 9.27	FG2028	Morris	?	?	B14	ex Bernard, to Dunf Tmys, to Alexander (O134)
7.28	FG4294	Albion PKA26	5068G	Alexander	B26F	to Dunf Tmys, to Alexander (C184)
aq 6.30	UH6759	Albion PMB28	?	North Counties	B30R	ex Demonstrator, to Alexander (E9)

108. *This Albion demonstrator (UH 6759) was obtained by John Turner of Kelty just a year before his business was taken over by Alexander. Left: R. Henderson. Right: P. McConnell.*

WEST FIFESHIRE MOTOR SERVICE CO LTD
J Murray Clubb, 23 & 42 James Street, Dunfermline

Livery: Grey

Used Philp's back yard and may have acquired Philp's business in January 1917. An ambitious series of routes was attempted, from Dunfermline to Saline and Steelend, Blairhall, Charlestown, Rosyth and Donibristle. Business abandoned December 1918 'owing to cars being under repair resulting from the state of the roads'.

Vehicles:

12.16	SP2890	?	?	?	?	ni
7.17	SP2971	?	?	?	?	ni

WEST'S
David West, 27 Pitcairn Street, Dunfermline

Livery: Red (some Green)

Road haulage business founded by David West, former driver with the ABC Co. Ex-Army chassis with convertible lorry/bus bodies were owned. A route from Dunfermline to Burntisland via Aberdour was run from May 1924, then Dunfermline to Limekilns from August 1925. The bus side of the business was allowed to lapse with concentration on the haulage side – which still trades today (one of few links with the pioneering bus days). One bus named 'Red Robin'.

Vehicles

aq 5.24	SP3220	Karrier WDS	2727	Jackson?	B34	ex Saline MS 5.24
aq .24	SP5667	Karrier	2905	Jackson	B30	ex Jack
?	SP5718	Karrier WDS	1734	Jackson	?	ni
?	?	Karrier	?	Jackson	?	ni

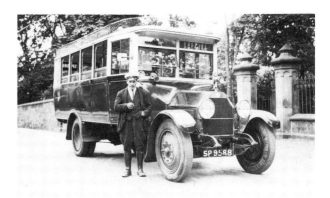

109. *Young's third bus was this Crerar-bodied Lancia SP 8415 which ran Lochgelly – Dunfermline. Note the spare tyre on the roof!*

110. *Lancia SP 9588 had a 26-seat body by Strachan & Brown of London. No fleet number had then been allocated.*

111. *Happy group of Young's employees, in Dunfermline. Bus No 13 on the right was Young's only Thornycroft (FG 5169).*

112. *All Leyland FG 5206 was new in July 1929, when it was photographed in Oakfield, Kelty. It, and others like it, soon spelled the death knell of the Kelty trams.*

113. *Leyland FG 4757 at the Tay Street stance in Perth with an unusual full-fronted body by Cadogan.*

114. *Young's highest numbered bus, No 20 was Leyland FG 6975, new in May 1931; to Alexander just four months later. The view, in Tay Street, Perth, can therefore be quite accurately dated.*

Livery: Dark Red (some early vehicles Grey)

Bus operator from c July 1922, previously having run a taxi service to Rosyth Dockyard. Commenced operating Kelty – Kirkcaldy via Cowdenbeath (reversing) and Lochgelly, then Kelty to Dunfermline via Gask and Wellwood. A Cowdenbeath to Perth run started in May 1929 was extended to Dunfermline in September 1929. A further service linked Cowdenbeath and Burntisland. Acquired the businesses of Turnbull in November 1922 and Davidson in March 1928. Working combine formed with Baxter and Kelty MT Co in May 1931. Purchased by Alexander September 1931.

Vehicles:

		Reg	Make	Chassis	Body	Seat	Notes
	7.22	SP7169	Guy	08022	?	Ch20	Sold 5.24
	12.23	SP8414	Reliance	?	Bristol	B?	Sold 5.28
	12.23	SP8415	Lancia	227E	Crerar	B20F	Sold 10.27 (licence F3)
	3.24	MS2893	Seddon	?	?	B20	ni
	5.24	SP9042	Lancia	232	?	B20	Sold 2.32 (licence F5)
	11.24	SP9588	Lancia	?	Strachan & Brown	B26F	(licence F6)
	12.24	SP9630	Reo	?	?	B14	Ser 4.32 (licence F4)
	6.25	FG 492	Reo	?	?	B20	(licence F1)
	12.25	FG1077	Reo	?	?	B26	Ser 3.31 (licence F2)
	aq 8.26	XN4650	Lancia	?	Hickman	B20F	ni
	5.27	FG3025	Minerva	27637	?	B32	To Alexander (?)
	6.27	GD6897	Gilford	?	?	B32F	ni
1	10.27	FG3487	Leyland PLSC	46276	Leyland	B36F	To Alexander (L76)
	aq 3.28	SP9738	Lancia	?	?	B20	ex Davidson sold 9.29
	aq 3.28	VA3903	Lancia	?	?	B26F	ex Davidson to Alexander (?)
	4.28	FG3905	Guy	50057	?	B14	To Alexander (O210)
	aq 5.28	FG1429	De Dion	410	?	B20	ex Sharp sold 11.28
2	7.28	FG4318	Leyland PLSC	47432?	?	B32F	To Alexander (L77)
3	10.28	FG4429	Leyland PLSC	47653	Dickson	B32F	To Alexander (L78)
4	3.29	FG4757	Leyland PLSC	46839	Cadogan	B..F	To Alexander (L79)
13	6.29	FG5169	Thornycroft	17775	?	B20F	To Alexander (O211)
12?	7.29	FG5206	Leyland LT1	50136	Leyland	B30R	To Alexander (N130)
14	7.29	FG5249	Albion PKA26	5086H	Pickering	B25F	To Alexander (C207)
15?	8.29	FG5372	AEC Reliance	660327	Dickson	B30	To Alexander (O205)
16?	8.29	FG5397	Leyland LT1	50499	Leyland	B30F	To Alexander (N131)
19?	3.30	FG5878	AEC Regal	662256	Dickson	C32	To Alexander (O206)
17	5.30	FG6093	AEC Regal	662257	Dickson	C32	To Alexander (O207)
18	12.30	FG6543	Leyland TS1	61423	Leyland	B32F	To Alexander (P108)
20	5.31	FG6975	Leyland TS1	61724	Leyland	B32F	To Alexander (P107)

115. *Young's Lancia XN 4650 tackles the Devil's Elbow on a Braemar Games excursion trip. This was a severe test for both vehicles and driver in the twenties.*

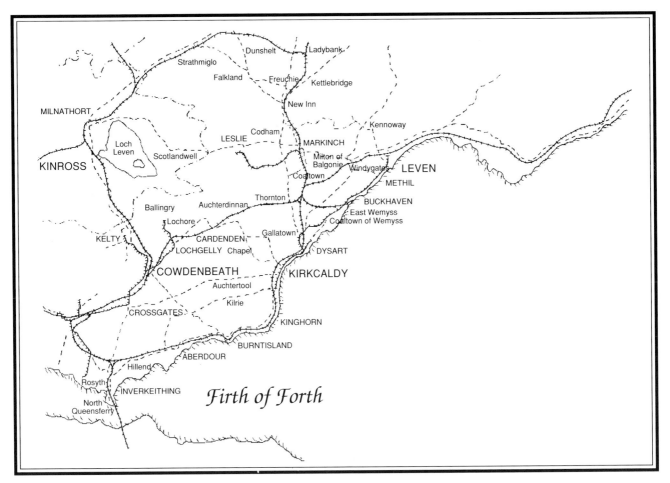

116. *Map of bus routes around Kirkcaldy.*

117. *Fife's best known vintage bus – Leven's 'Buckie Bus' did not even belong to the Kingdom! The body had been a Leyland owned by McCallum & Graham of Dundee and was used to and from Kirriemuir before the chassis was purchased by ex-Provost Anderson of Leven for further use. The body, which gradually acquired even more buckies – or shells – was decorated by William Bisset over the ensuing years.*

3. BUS OPERATORS - EAST FIFE

ANDREW'S — Robert Andrew, Commercial Road, Leven

Horse bus proprietor who purchased his first motor bus in April 1921, operating from Leven to Glenlomond Sanitorium. Business taken over by Harris (q.v.) of Leven who also took over the premises – which had originally been known as Caledonian Stables.

Vehicles:

4.21	?	Albion	?	?	Ch	ni
6.22	?	Albion ?	?	?	B14	ni

A & R MOTOR SERVICES (BUCKHAVEN) LTD — Thomas Anderson and James Roden, Buckhaven

Livery: Chocolate Brown

Incorporated as a limited company 17 April 1926 to acquire and operate the business of T Anderson (trading as Buckhaven Motor Carrying Co). Jas Roden was a local cinema owner with no other omnibus interest. Operated as 'chasers' to the Wemyss Trams between Kirkcaldy (Gallatown) and Leven. Control purchased May 1927 by Wemyss Tramway Co who placed their nominees on the board. Continued operating as a nominally separate undertaking until acquired on 20 June 1930 by W Alexander & Sons with the other Companies under control of Wemyss Tramway Co. Five vehicles sold to GMC on 14 June 1932 for £2226.

Vehicles:

aq 4.26	FG987	Reo	W1720	?	B24F	ex Buckhaven Motor Co
aq 4.26	FG989	Reo	?	?	B24F	ex Buckhaven Motor Co
aq 4.26	FG991	Reo	1540	?	B20F	ex Buckhaven Motor Co
5.26	GD2557	Reo	?	?	B24F	ni
5.26	GD2558	Reo	?	?	B24F	ni
8.26	FG2175	?	?	?	?	ni sold 7.31

BIRRELL — John Birrell, High Street, Markinch

Livery: Yellow and Red

Verbal reports only of operations from Markinch to Leven, using 'Reo and Lancias'. No further information available at present on operation of regular services, but tours to St Andrews were undertaken.

Vehicles:

?	?	Reo	?	?	ch/ly	ni
?	?	Lancia	?	?	B/ly	ni

118. *Reo FG 991 of 'A & R Pullman Motor Safety Coaches', formerly with Buckhaven Motor Company, on the Kirkcaldy to Leven route.*

119. *Ford Model 'T' SP 9979 of Finlay Brown, illustrating what the best dressed crew of 1925 were wearing.*

120. *Brown's later buses were smart Albions, shown in this maker's photo of – probably – FG 5781.*

FINLAY BROWN

Livery: Red, Yellow (Ford was Grey)

Commenced operation in 1923, running Windygates – Leven via Methilhill and Crossroads, this was extended through to Kennoway. Business of A Houston acquired December 1929. By 1931 routes were also being run to Cupar and Newport from Leven. Purchased by Alexander 11 October 1931.

Vehicles:

?	?	?	?	?	ch/ly	ni
3.25	SP9979	Ford	?	?	B14F	ni
?	?	Bean	?	?	B14	ni
?	?	Reo	?	?	?	ni
10.28	FG4474	Albion PKA26	5069B	?	B26F	to GMC, to Alexander (C201)
7.29	FG5268	Albion PKA26	5087I	?	?	to GMC, to Alexander (C202)
aq 12.29	VA2973	Reo	?	?	B14F	ex Houston
aq 12.29	FG1774	Chevrolet	X8677	?	B14F	ex Houston
aq 12.29	FG2255	Reo	?	?	B20	ex Houston
aq 12.29	SN3545	Albion PJ24	?	?	B24	ex Houston
aq 12.29	UI1928	Albion PM28	7018B	?	B32R	ex Houston to Cormie
aq 12.29	FG4585	Albion PKA26	5069I	?	B26F	ex Houston
6.30	FG5781	Albion PMA28	7057B	?	B32F	to GMC, to Alexander (D58)
aq 30	OF7099	Albion PMA28	7057F	?	B32F	ex Demonstrator to GMC, to W A (D56)
7.30	FG6208	Albion PMA28	7066A	?	?	to GMC, to Alexander (D59)
5.31	FG6946	Albion PMA28	7066D	?	?	to GMC, to Alexander (D57)

HARRY K BROWN

May for a short time have operated between Thornton Station and Thornton Village. No other records.

Vehicle:

c 1920	SP5139	Ford 'T'	?	?	?	ni

BUCKHAVEN MOTOR CARRYING CO

Livery: Blue

Commenced business on 12 May 1922 – the first 'chasers' of the Wemyss Tramways running from Leven to Gallatown v. East Wemyss. Reconstituted from 17 April 1926 as the A & R Motor Services (Buckhaven) Co Ltd q.v.

Vehicles:

5.22	?	Ford	?	?	?	ni
?	?	?	?	?	?	sold 3.25
?	SP 827	?	?	?	?	sold 5.25
1.25	SP9709	?	?	?	?	sold 3.26 to Harrow & Stocks
12.25	FG 987	Reo	W1720	?	B24F	To A & R MS
12.25	FG 989	Reo	?	?	B24F	To A & R MS
12.25	FG 991	Reo	1540	?	B20F	To A & R MS

BURNETT

Only reference is in Leven Advertiser of 17 November 1909 '. . . A large motor omnibus last week put on the road . . .'. It operated from Largo through Leven and Windygates to Kennoway. Nothing is known of its success or for how long it was operated.

CAIRNS

Is said to have operated between Dysart and West Wemyss in 1922. No further information.

CALEY BUS COMPANY

First motor bus operation, Leven to Anstruther via Largo and Colinsburgh commenced 1 October 1920, followed in June 1922 by a route from Leven to Kennoway via Windygates. The business was incorporated as a limited company on 19 October 1920. Competition with the Wemyss Tramway commenced (Leven to Gallatown) on 20 November 1923. To compensate the effect upon their income the Wemyss Tramway Co bought out its competitors, acquiring as part of that policy the 'Caley' on 23 April 1925. Continued trading as a nominally separate Company, but concentrating on private car hire, still using the Mitchell Street premises until acquisition along with the rest of the Wemyss' controlled companies by Alexander, effective 20 June 1930. Limited Company wound up 1 March 1932.

Vehicles:

4.20	SP 24	Belsize	?	?	Ch	sold 4.23
4.20	SP4224	Belsize	?	?	Ch	Ser 9.31
7.20	SP4411	Selden?	?	?	?	ni
9.20	SP4886	Tilling-Stevens?	?	?	?	To Wemyss Tmy 11.26 Scr 10.28
2.21	SP5090	Halley ?	?	?	?	Ser 12.25
6.21	SP6106	Daimler?	?	?	?	To Wemyss Tmy 1.30 To Alexander 1.32
aq 4.25	SP8343	Daimler	?	?	?	ex Campbell, Leven, to Wemyss Tmys 4.26

Livery: Cream below waist Deep Blue above, Black mudguards (original livery was all white with black mudguards)

Ran lorries (Overland 12 cwt) carrying explosives to local coal mines. Opened bus services in Aberdeenshire (to Tarland and Dunecht — sold to Alexander 1932) and in Montrose (to Forfar, Bervie and Ferryden) in July 1926. Montrose routes sold to Northern General Omnibus Co in December 1927, but two buses retained to open service in Kirkcaldy. This was one of the first services (opened 23 December 1927) to challenge the Corporation's refusal to allow buses to compete within the boundaries with its tramways. After this successful enterprise others followed, the ultimate result being closure of the tramways, prior to which Cormie had offered (unsuccessfully) to purchase the tramways from the Corporation. Rapid expansion followed, with some disruption when a garage fire in January 1930 destroyed four buses (including 2 Crossley and 1 Albion).

Incorporated as limited liability company on 4 November 1930. First double deck bus in Fife obtained as demonstrator but not licenced. Prestige Glasgow route run off road by Alexander following refusal of initial takeover proposed, whereupon route to Dunfermline commenced. Next approach by Alexander was accepted and the business transferred, effective 11 October 1931. The Company was then put into voluntary liquidation. After ceasing bus operations, for some years Cormie operated 'Majestic Transport' using AEC Magestic trucks, later with AEC Mammoth and Major types.

Routes:

Kirk Wynd — Gallatown ('Kirkcaldy Bus Service') commenced 23 December 1927

Whytescauseway — Dysart via Dunnikier Road (January 1928) — extended to West Wemyss (July 1928)

Burntisland — Leven (November 1928) became Aberdour — Lundin Links (June 1929) which in January 1930 became Glasgow to Lundin Links via Stirling (a journey which took 4 hours). This was replaced in January 1931 by a Dunfermline to Leven only service.

Kirkcaldy — Perth operated from mid 1928.

Vehicles:

aq c .27	?	Morris	?	?	B12F	ni
aq c .27	SR6229	Reo	745229	?	B14F	to Alexander (O192)
6.27	FG3132	Star	B558	?	B20	ni
1.28	GD9812	Reo	GB111	Mitchell	B26F	to Alexander (O197)
1.28	FG3698	Reo	?	Mitchell	B32	to Brodie, to SMT
2.28	FG3730	Reo	GB126	?	B26	Ser 3.28
aq ?	?	Dennis	?	?	B20	ni
9.28	FG4426	Maudslay ML4B	4443	?	B26	to Alexander (O186)
10.28	FG4427	Maudslay ML4B	4444	?	B26	to Alexander (O185)
10.28	FG4467	Dennis G	70413	?	?	to Alexander (O176)
10.28	FG4468	Dennis G	?	?	?	to Alexander (O177)
10.28	FG4486	?	?	?	?	sold 7.30
3.29	FG4702	Maudslay ML3B	4469	?	B28	to Alexander (O184)
3.29	FG4703	Maudslay ML3B	4497	?	B28	to Alexander (O183)
4.29	FG4894	Maudslay ML4B	4552	?	?	to Alexander (O182)
4.29	FG4895	Maudslay ML4B	4551	?	?	to Alexander (O181)
5.29	FG4961	Crossley Eagle	90031	Eaton	?	to Alexander (O173)
9.29	FG5370	Crossley	?	?	?	sold 4.30
9.29	FG5371	Crossley Alpha	90204	Dickson	B30	to Alexander (O169)
10.29	FG5468	Chevrolet LQ	59093	?	?	to Alexander (O190)
10.29	FG5621	Crossley Alpha	90223	Dickson	?	to Alexander (O170)
1.30	MY2421	AEC Regal	662553	?	?	ex Demonstrator to Alexander (O187)
3.30	FG5853	Maudslay ML6	4810	?	?	to Alexander (O180)
3.30	FG5854	Maudslay ML6	4811	?	?	to Alexander (O179)
7.30	FG6225	Crossley Alpha	90249	Taylor	B32	to Alexander (O167)
aq ?	TX3858	Albion PM28	7011A	?	?	orig. Griffiths to Alexander (C198)
aq .30	UI1928	Albion PM28	7018B	?	B26	orig. Londonderry Cpn. to Alexander (C200)
aq ?	UI2050	Albion PM28	7037K	?	B32R	orig. Londonderry Cpn. to Alexander (C199)
aq .30	VM5789	Crossley Eagle	90010	Arnold	?	ex Demonstrator
aq .30	VR4832	Crossley Arrow	90208	Crossley	?	ex Demonstrator
aq .30	VR9008	Crossley Alpha	90274	Crossley	?	ex Demonstrator to Alexander (O168)
8.30	FG6351	Crossley Alpha	90288	Dickson	?	to Alexander (O166)
8.30	FG6352	Crossley Alpha	90287	Dickson	?	to Alexander (O165)
2.31	FG6648	Ford AA	3959715	?	B20	to Alexander (O189)
aq ?	FG5468	Chevrolet LQ	59093	?	?	ex Davidson, Kirkcaldy (orig Central Garage, Cupar)

Vehicles in Alexanders fleet list but probably operated by GMC up to 1938

'Platform Promises' from the Press of November 1929.

121. *Cormie's Reo FG 3698 was sold to Brodie of Harthill who operated to Bathgate.*

122. *Cormie operated several Maudslays. This one, FG 5853 was photographed in Glasgow on the long route through Stirling to Leven.*

DRYBURGH'S
Andrew Dryburgh, Coaltown of Wemyss

Commenced operation in July 1922, running from Dysart to Leven via East Wemyss. A Dryburgh was later an employee of GMC, so the business may have been acquired by them.

Vehicle:

6.22	SP7063	Napoleon-Seabrook	?	?	Ch	ni

FERNIE'S
Jas Fernie, Auchtertool

Commenced operation in December 1923, running Saturdays and Sundays only from Kirkcaldy to Cowdenbeath via Auchtertool. Convertible lorry with charabanc body for weekend use. Not known how long operation continued.

Vehicle:

aq c 12.23	?	Thornycroft	?	?	ch/lry	ni

FLEMING
Peter Fleming, Bonnybank, Kennoway

Commenced operation in 1922, weekend only service using lorry converted to charabanc; running Kennoway to Leven. Not known how long operation continued.

Vehicle:

aq c .22	?	Maudslay	?	?	ch/lry	ni

FRASER
Alex Fraser, Leslie

Short-lived operation from Leslie to Kirkcaldy.

Vehicle:

4.21	SP5183	Maudslay	?	?	?	ni

Livery: Red and White

Established 1922 but first regular service established c 1925. Business acquired by Alexander 15 January 1932 and passed for operational purposes to GMC. Sixteen vehicles reported to have been in fleet at time of transfer but only five are listed in surviving records.

Routes:

Anstruther to St Andrews via Crail, became Elie to Newport via Anstruther and St Andrews, extended in 1929 to become Leven to Newport via Coast.

Anstruther to St Andrews via Dunino.

St Andrews Town Service (Market Street – Lomond Drive) operated for one summer only, not repeated as not profitable.

Vehicles:

5.25	FG 386	Morris	?	?	ch14	ni
5.25	FG 396	Morris	?	?	ch14	ni
10.25	FG 903	Lancia	970	Crerar	B26	ni
3.26	FG1309	Lancia G4	1207	Crerar	B26	ni
4.26	FG1653	Lancia	332	Crerar	ch18	to GMC (O156)
7.26	FG2056	Minerva	?	Park Royal	B?F	to GMC (O158)
6.27	FG3149	Thornycroft	?	Grant Cameron & Curle	B32F	ni
7.25	ES7786	De Dion	880	Crerar	B25F	ex Crerar, Crieff to GMC (O159)
7.25	ES7939	De Dion	?	Crerar	B25F	ex Crerar, Crieff
aq .30	CK4165	Leyland LT1	50167	?	B32F	ex Watkinson Preston, to GMC (N126)
aq .30	CK4166	Leyland LT1	50168	?	B32F	ex Watkinson Preston, to GMC (N127)
6.30	FG6130	Thornycroft	?	?	B F	ni

NB Three additional Thornycrofts are stated to have been owned. The two Leylands reputedly first diesel fuelled buses in Fife.

123. *Gardner's first two Morris charabancs outside the original garage, at Harbourhead.*

124. *At Harbourhead, left to right, Lancia FG 1653, De Dion ES 7939, Lancias FG 1309 and FG 903.*

125. *Lancia charabanc FG 1653 when new. What was Gardner's garage is now the very popular Fisheries Museum.*

126. *The first Thornycroft, FG 3149, a 32-seater with bodywork by Grant Cameron and Curle of Glasgow. Driver A Gillespie.*

127. *The last purchase was FG 6130, photographed at the 1927 garage built in Pittenweem Road.*

128. *Auchterderran Road, Lochgelly was the locus of this scene. The Caledon make was first marketed in 1915, GMC buying them in large numbers over the ensuring years. This one is probably S 4952.*

129. *Record shot of GMC No 36, Commer FG 3953 of 1928, illustrating the vast improvement in vehicle design in just over a decade.*

Above left:
130. *One of the first Commer buses photographed in Burntisland, the first route to be operated by the Company, from July 1913.*

Above:
131. *At least five Commers were owned by May 1914, but this one, with a charabanc body, was photographed in Kirkcaldy High Street after the First World War.*

Left:
132. *Caledon No 5 of the GMC fleet was SP 5798, photographed in Thistle Street. The blue saltire radiator badge was an instantly recognisable symbol. J M Barclay (right) served with Alexander until retirement. D Brand on the left.*

Left:
133. *Gleneagles Golfcourse, July 1923. The Caledon charabanc TS 3093 was registered in Dundee by the Will Motor Transport Company, passing to GMC in September 1922.*

Below left:
134. *Caledon SP 5843 (No 23), now 'modernised' with pneumatic tyres, Sands Road, Kirkcaldy c1924.*

Below:
135. *Record photo by J Stewart, body-builder of AEC, SP 8977. The top half of the body could be lifted off to convert to a charabanc-style vehicle.*

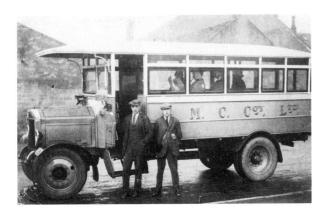

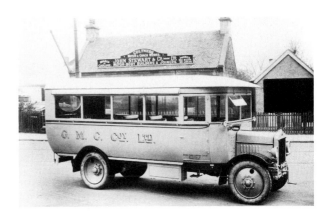

Livery: Slate Grey; c 1930 some vehicles Red and Cream (as SGO Co); after c 1932 'Alexander' Blue

Sturrock and McGregor (brothers-in-law) started in business as haulage contractors in Kirkcaldy and Leith for Todd's flour mill. Weekend tours were run with charabanc bodies on the lorry chasses. First service commenced July 1913 from Kirkcaldy (West Bridge) – by the Links tram terminus – to Burntisland via Kinghorn. Services to Lochgelly and to Leslie followed prior to a general retrenchment caused by the First World War. Operations were reduced and several vehicles, of a fleet which consisted of Commers and Caledons, were converted to run on town gas with canvas gas holders mounted on the vehicle's roof. In 1913 John McGregor lived in Kinghorn in the home of Robert Forrester, later pioneer of bus operations in the Lochgelly area.

Development resumed after cessation of hostilities and a limited liability company was registered on 1 December 1919 with 20,000 shares of £1 each. The two pioneers were paid £16,000 in shares of the new business. Additional directors were James and Angus McGregor. At this time a new Company, Scottish Utility Motors was formed by Sturrock and McGregor, to act as motor dealers and general carriers. The two companies operated closely, with many buses passing through the books of the Utility Motor Company, a large number being rebuilt for commercial use in the process. All evidence suggests that, surprisingly neither company constructed bus bodywork.

A period of rapid expansion followed with several new routes opened. In 1918 control of the Dunfermline based ABC Company was obtained but no effort appears to have been made to continue operations in this area, the ABC Company being wound up. In 1921 an interest was taken in the Will Motor Transport Co Ltd of Dundee (incorporated in 1919 by a local coal merchant and operating services to Alyth and Tealing). This could have resulted from an indebtedness incurred over supply of vehicles, some of which were taken into the GMC fleet after the Will MT Co was wound up in September 1922. During 1924 an interest was taken in the Gala Motor Transport Co of Galashiels (later Lanark). This undertaking had been founded by Mr Robert Wilson who later went on to form the still flourishing bus operating company based in Carnwath. Some vehicle interchange took place, with the 'C' of GMC on the side of the bus quickly and simply changed to a 'T' for GMT.

During 1923 GMC started operating services from a new base in St Andrews. Buses were driven up from Kirkcaldy each day – and back at night – until a garage was built in Grange Road.

By 1925 the GMC fleet was recorded as 37 vehicles, an assortment of 20 Caledons, 4 Commers, 3 Leylands, 1 Halley, 2 Daimlers and 7 AEC, but this grew and changed so that the next year the number of buses was recorded as 56.

In 1926, however, a controlling interest in GMC was purchased by the Wemyss Tramway Company as a major part of their acquisition policy to combat competition with their major investment in the tramway. As part of the Balfour Beatty power and traction empire, the competitors with the trams had to be contained. Although two Wemyss nominees (Messrs Dawson and Murray) were put on the board to replace Angus and James McGregor, the co-founders remained very much in control and the Company acted independently, although wasteful duplication was eliminated. The Tramway Company also operated their own vehicles on their own routes.

Purchase by the Wemyss Company brought the GMC Co into a large – but fragmented – omnibus group which formed the bus operating division of the Fife Tramway Light and Power Co Ltd (Balfour Beatty owned also). The major constituent was the Scottish General Omnibus Company of Larbert – originally the bus department of the Falkirk Tramways – who had achieved a foothold in Fife by the purchase of T & J Cousins of Culross in 1925; the bus department of the Dunfermline Tramways, plus A & R Motors and the Caley Motor Co. Considerable interchange of vehicles amongst group members took place. By the end of 1927 a fleet of 83 buses had been accumulated.

This period of expansion included the opening of a route to Perth in December 1927 and a through service (jointly operated with the Scottish General Omnibus Co) to Glasgow one year later. Access to an alternative route to Perth was obtained by a joint operation with Fullers Motors of Newburgh whose small business was purchased in 1929.

Also in 1929 Alex Sturrock assumed a controlling interest in the Glen Motor Transport Co of Fraserburgh. This illustrates well the convoluted nature of the bus industry of this period; a holding in Glen was also owned by the Gala Motor Transport Company and separately by Robert Wilson individually.

Soon after, in June 1930, Balfour Beatty sold their Fife bus operations to Alexanders, acting as the holding company for SMT. The existing board of directors was replaced in total, by Walter Alexander, W Alexander Junior and Wm Thomson. Scottish Utility Motors also passed to Alexander and was quickly wound up, in 1932. GMC however continued as a 'named' company, the operating base for Alexander in East Fife. Vehicles were numbered in a combined Alexander list from 1931-32 although carrying a 'General' livery. GMC was wound up in 1937 and the 'General' name lapsed in 1938. The two pioneers were not finished, however, and formed a new Company in 1930, Sturrock and McGregor Ltd to act as vehicle dealers and general contractors. This enterprise was taken over by Scottish Roadways in 1934.

Routes:

    Kirkcaldy (West Bridge) – Burntisland (7.13) – Aberdour (6.21)
    Kirkcaldy (Nicol Street) – Kinglassie via Cardenden (9.13) Abandoned 8.14
    Kirkcaldy (Gallatown) – Thornton (10.13) Abandoned 8.14
    Kirkcaldy (Nicol Street) – Lochgelly via Cardenden (12.13)
    Kirkcaldy (Nicol Street) – Leslie via Thornton and Markinch (9.14)
    Kirkcaldy (Gallatown) – Falkland (2.20) – Auchtermuchty (5.20) – Perth via Gateside (12.27-7.29)
    Kirkcaldy (Charlotte Street) – Dunfermline via Kilrie, Donibristle and Crossgates (5.21)
    Kirkcaldy (Gallatown) – Pitlessie via Freuchie and Kingskettle (11.21-12.21 only)
    Kirkcaldy (Gallatown) – Windygates via Coaltown of Balgonie (11.21) – Leven (5.22)
    – Windygates (from 6.22 after agreement with Caley M Co) – Cupar via Kennoway (7.26)
    Kirkcaldy terminus for all routes (except Lochgelly) becomes Sands Road (Esplanade) from 29.10.23
    St Andrews – Anstruther via Crail (6.23)
    St Andrews – Cupar via Blebo – Kirkcaldy via Markinch (4.28)
    St Andrews – Anstruther via Kingsbarns (10.26)
    Kirkcaldy – Auchtertool (3.27) – Cowdenbeath (11.27)
    Kirkcaldy Town Service (Kirk Wynd – Gallatown via Dunnikier Road and Overton Road) (12.27)
    Kirkcaldy – Glasgow via Donibristle, Dunfermline and Stirling (12.28) joint with Scottish General
    Kirkcaldy – Perth via Auchtermuchty and Newburgh (7.29) originally joint with Fullers Motors

Vehicles:

Early buses were named: 'Seafield Castle', 'Dunnikier Castle', 'Rosslyn Castle', 'Ravenscraig Castle', 'Balwerie Castle', 'Rossend Castle', 'Wemyss Castle', 'Abbotshall Castle', 'Raith Castle', 'Cumbernauld Castle' (?).

	7.13	?	Commer	?	?	ch	ni
		?	Commer	?	?	ch	ni
		?	Commer	?	?	ch	ni
		?	Commer	?	?	ch	ni
	5.14	?	Commer	?	?	ch28	ni
	3.15	S4952	Caledon	?	?	B?R	ni
	.17	S7882	Caledon	?	?	B?R	ni
	?	GA3585	Caledon	?	?	?	ni
14	.17	S 7950	Caledon	?	?	B?F	ni
17	.18	S 8148	Caledon	?	?	B?F	ni
18	?	SP1921	Caledon	?	?	B32R	Scr 12.36
	.19	SP3648	Caledon	?	?	B32R	Scr 12.36
	.20	SP4885	Caledon	?	?	?	Scr 9.41
9	.20	SG 156	Caledon	?	?	B32R	ni
	.20	SG 421	Caledon	?	?	B32R	ni
	3.21	SP5721	Fiat	?	?	?	Scr 12.36
	3.21	SP5722	Fiat	?	?	?	ni
	3.21	SP5723	Fiat	?	?	?	ni
	3.21	SP5724	Fiat	?	?	?	To Peric M Co Edinburgh 5.23 Scr 11.36
5	4.21	SP5798	Caledon	?	?	B32R	Scr 1.31
15	4.21	SP5799	Commer	RC5206	?	ch	to Sturrock & McGregor
	4.21	SP5800	Caledon	?	?	24	Scr 9.30
22	5.21	SP5842	Caledon	?	?	B32F	Scr 12.36
23	5.21	SP5843	Caledon	E626	?	B32F	Scr 9.30
24	5.21	SP5941	Caledon	?	?	ch29	ni
	5.21	SP5947	Fiat	?	?	ch14	Scr 12.36
	6.21	SP6124	Albion	H1806	?	?	ni
	6.21	SP6125	Albion	?	?	?	To Sc Utility Motors 1.25 Scr 6.33
	.21	SG4066	Daimler	?	?	26	ni
	.21	SG4355	Daimler	?	?	32	ni
	7.21	SP6212	Daimler	?	?	B30R	Scr 12.36
	9.21	SP6373	Albion	?	?	?	ni
	4.22	SP6833	Thornycroft	?	?	26	ni
	5.22	SP6967	Commer	?	?	26	ni
aq 9.22		TS2201	Caledon	?	?	ch32	ex Will MT Co, Dundee, new 3.20
aq 9.22		TS2954	Caledon	?	?	?	ex Will MT Co, Dundee, new 2.21
32 aq 9.22		TS2977	Caledon	?	?	?	ex Will MT Co, Dundee, new 3.21
29 aq 9.22		TS3093	Caledon	?	?	ch	ex Will MT Co, Dundee, new 5.21
aq 9.22		TS3168	Caledon	?	?	ch32	ex Will MT Co, Dundee, new 6.21
	1.23	SP7434	Caledon	?	?	29	Scr 12.36
	5.23	SP7915	Guy	?	?	ch14	Scr 9.31
	6.23	SP7988	AEC	?	?	B26	ni
	6.23	SP8027	Caledon	?	?	26	To Gala MT 6.23 To GMC 6.27, Scr 1.31
	1.24	SP8452	AEC	?	?	ch32	Scr 11.31
	1.24	SP8510	AEC	?	?	ch32	To Sturrock & McGregor 11.30
26	4.24	SP8727	Chevrolet	?	?	ch14	Scr 12.36
	5.24	SP8883	?	?	?	ch14	Scr 12.36
	5.24	SP8977	AEC	202004	Stewart	B?F	ni
	5.24	SP9008	?	?	?	?	Scr 12.36
	5.24	SP9009	?	?	?	?	To Sc Utility Motors 11.26
30	7.24	SP9294	Chevrolet	?	?	ch14	Sold 5.30
	1.25	SP9659	Leyland A13	35299	?	B24	Scr 9.37 (Alexander K17)
	4.25	SP9832	Halley	?	?	B20R	Sold 7.31
	4.25	SP9833	Leyland	35404	?	B32R	ni
	4.25	SP9864	GMC	162545S	?	ch14	Scr 3.29
	4.25	SP9985	Caledon	?	?	26	Scr 12.36
	5.25	FG 52	Leyland A13	35436	?	B26	Sold 12.32 (Alexander K16)
	6.25	FG 186	Caledon	?	?	ch32	ni
1	10.25	FG 915	AEC202	202005	Strachan & Brown	32	ni
	?	V6817	Commer	?	?	ch32	ni
	?	EL6334	AEC	?	?	ch32	ni
	?	SD5774	Commer	?	?	30	ni
aq 26		SP6119	Thornycroft	6151	SMT	B32	ex SGO Co ex Cousins
aq 26		NW3563	Thornycroft	9733	Strachan & Brown	B35	ex SGO Co ex Cousins
aq 26		SP7036	Lothian	?	SMT	B32R	ex SGO Co ex Cousins
aq 26		SP9372	Lothian	?	SMT	B32R	ex SGO Co ex Cousins
	5.26	FG1658	Albion PJ24	4138I	?	?	Sold 8.33 (Alexander B22)
55	5.26	FG1659	Albion PJ24	4138H	?	B?F	Sold .33 (Alexander B7)

136. *Driver Walter Price with Halley SP 9832 at the Sands Road stance Kirkcaldy. Behind is Smith's Studebaker No 18.*

137. *Purchased at the same time as the bus shown above was this large Leyland with a 32-seat body, SP 9833. Photographed in Charlotte Street, Kirkcaldy, 1925.*

138. *Outing to Crieff by the Pathhead & Sinclairtown Co-op in GMC's Caledon No 60, Dumfries registered SM 5131. Behind is, by comparison, a diminutive Chevrolet No 26, SP 8727, August 1927.*

139. *Commer FG 4123 at the Kirkcaldy stance, running to Perth via Kinross. It was new in May 1928.*

140. *Soft-top Commer No 66 was FG 4885, seen on a dismal day in Tay Street, Perth – probably in 1929.*

141. *Totally different body style on Commer FG 4931, also dating from 1929. The two vehicles show differing styles of the fleet name.*

17	5.26	FG1660	Albion PJ24	4141E	?	?	Sold .32 (Alexander B6)
	5.26	FG1661	Albion PJ24	4141F	?	24	Sold 9.33 (Alexander B23)
	5.26	FG1670	Chevrolet X	8752	?	ch14	ni
	5.26	FG1671	Chevrolet X	?	?	ch14	Scr 3.31
	5.26	FG1672	Chevrolet X	?	?	ch14	Sold 1.34
53	5.26	FG1673	Albion PF24	4078L	?	ch20	Sold 1.35 (Alexander B21)
52	5.26	FG1674	Bean	11245	?	ch14	(Alexander O133)
20	6.26	FG1846	Albion PF26	5000C	?	?	Sold .37 (Alexander C187)
58	7.26	FG1889	Albion PK26	5006L	?	B26F	Sold .37 (Alexander C193)
57	7.26	FG1890	Albion PK26	5010F	?	B26F	Sold .38 (Alexander C194)
59	7.26	FG1891	Albion PK26	5010E	?	B26F	Sold .38 (Alexander C186)
60	?	SM5131	Caledon	?	?	ch32	ni
	5.27	FG2877	Thornycroft	13471	?	32	ni
44	5.27	FG3088	Thornycroft	?	?	18	Sold 5.32
2	6.27	FG3128	Commer	?	?	?	To Gala MT Co 6.27
24	1.28	FG3645	Commer 4GN	6539	?	B30	To Saline MS 6.28
	3.28	FG3880	Albion	?	?	26	Scr 12.36
	5.28	FG3952	Commer	?	?	?	Sold 1.33 (Alexander O147)
36	5.28	FG3953	Commer 4PN	19002	?	B28F	ni
37	5.28	FG3954	Commer 4PN	?	?	B28F	Sold 6.32
61	5.28	FG3955	Commer 30GP	11040	?	18	Sold to Robertson, Arran
62	5.28	FG3956	Commer 2PM	6508	?	?	ni
65	5.28	FG4081	Commer 30GP	11050	?	20	Alexander (O148)
63	5.28	FG4123	Commer G4	12018	?	B28F	ni
64	5.28	FG4124	Commer G4	12019	?	B28F	ni
	10.28	FG4422	ADC	426066	Hall Lewis	B28F	Alexander (O144)
22	3.29	FG4697	ADC	416608	Cowieson	B30F	Alexander (O142)
66	4.29	FG4885	Commer M4	15005	?	B28F	ni
29	4.29	FG4886	ADC	426038	?	B30F	(Alexander O143)
73	?	FG3360	Ford	14994844	?	?	ni
78	?	VA7076	Pagefield	?	?	32	New 11.27
80	5.29	FG4931	Commer 4PF	25004	Stewart	B32F	Sold .31
	6.29	FG5043	Gilford 1663D	10582	?	26	ni
18	?	GM1158	Gilford	?	?	?	ni
48	?	GD8572	Studebaker	3174060	?	?	new 10.27
	7.29	FG5227	Commer F4	16006	?	30	ni
	7.29	FG5281	Thornycroft	18296	?	24	ni
	?	SU2460	Commer	?	?	?	ex Northern General (Elgin)
	?	SN3545	Albion PJ24	?	?	?	ex Northern General (Elgin)
	?	HH3958	Minerva	26051	?	B31	ex Ribble MS
56	?	TD9221	Leyland	45483	Leyland	B26F	ex Furness M Co, to Alexander (M8)
	aq 6.30	MS5272	Leyland	?	Law	B36F	ex W Alexander
	aq 6.30	GD1721	Albion	4146G	?	B26F	ex Rankin new 2.26

After acquisition by the combine the following were allocated to GMC –

6.30	MS9734-MS9748 Leyland
	MS9789-MS9787 Albion
6.31	WG282-WG287 Leyland
	WG333 Gilford; WG 504-5 Bedford; WG538, 571, 572, 579 Albion PW65

Many vehicles added to GMC from other operators (q.v.); Fullers Motors 7.28 (four), Wemyss Tramways Co 6.30 (eleven), Harrow & Stocks 15.12.30 (three), T. Gardner 15.1.31 (five); Peattie Bros 13.5.31 (two); Smith Bros 1.6.31 (twelve); Baxter 16.9.31 (eight); Kelty MT Co 16.9.31 (fifteen); A & A Young 20.9.31 (fifteen); Finlay Brown 4.10.31 (seven); Cormie 19.10.31 (twenty-six) and Milton MS 1.9.32 (ten). Vehicles numbered into combined fleet with Alexander etc. during 1932.

142. *Odd man out in the 1931 allocation to GMC was this Gilford, WG 333, photographed at Shorehead, Leven with its original fleet number, 787, which it carried only until 1932 when it became Y30.*

143. *Thornycroft FG 5113 of Harris & Sons was photographed in 1931 in South Street, St Andrews with its youthful crew – driver David Johnston completed his career with Alexander's many years later.*

144. *Another Harris Thornycroft disputed right of way with a lorry full of – fortunately – empty beer bottles. FG 6998 was new in June 1931.*

145. *Harris's premises in Commercial Road Leven with staff, c1931.*

GLENDINNING'S MOTOR SERVICE
David Glendinning, Kinghorn

Livery: Dark Red

Established September 1923, operating between Kirkcaldy and Burntisland until acquired by Jack Brothers.

Vehicles:

c 9.23	?	W & G Du Cross	?	?	B14	ni
?	?	W & G Du Cross	?	?	B14	ni
?	?	Reo	?	?	?	ni

HARRIS' BUS SERVICE
James Harris & Sons, Commercial Road, Leven

Livery: Olive Green (dark below waist, light above)

Established by 1924 – but hires and tours only prior to 1928. Purchased business of Robert Andrew, Leven in 1924, and J Hay, Lundin Links c 1935. Last independent operator in the area, resisting until taken over by Alexander on 11 May 1939.

Routes:
Kirkcaldy – St Andrews via Colinsburgh (from 1.5.28) became Leven – St Andrews from 15.6.29 then Buckhaven – St Andrews (from 10.29)

Leven – Anstruther v. Colinsburgh and Arncrooch (former Hays route)

Vehicles:

5.25	FG 493	Halley	?	?	ch/bus	body ex Tod
4.28	FG3904	Morris	?	?	ch/lorry	ni
4.28	FG3938	Thornycroft	?	?	ch20	ni
6.28	FG4145	Reo	C9419	Crerar ?	B20F	ex Demonstrator
6.29	FG5113	Thornycroft A2	18488	Jackson ?	B20F	ni
5.30	FG6112	Commer	28031	Alexander	B20F	'The Green Goddess' to Alexander (O1)
6.31	FG6998	Thornycroft A2	18738	Cameron	B24F	to Alexander (T39)
6.31	FG6999	Bedford	113754	?	B14F	ni
11.31	FG7276	Thornycroft A12	20915	Jackson	B26F	to Alexander (T38)
7.32	FG7944	Thornycroft A10	22474	Jackson	B24F	to Alexander (T40)
5.33	FS5991	Thornycroft A14	22560	Westwood & Smith	B20F	ex Tait, Leith; to Alexander (T41)
5.35	AFG627	Thornycroft CD	24336	Cadogan	C32F	To Alexander (T42)
5.36	ASP911	Thornycroft EE	24671	?	C32F	to Alexander (T44)
5.36	BFG164	Albion PV67	16200B	?	C32F	to Alexander (E30)
3.37	BFG762	Thornycroft	26258	Cadogan	C20F	to Alexander (T43)
5.38	CSP111	Albion	25020A	Alexander	C26F	to Alexander (A19)
4.39	HTN133	Bedford	15530	NCB	C26F	to Alexander (W88)

HARROW & STOCKS
Harrow & Stocks, Invertiel Road, Kirkcaldy

Livery: Dark Blue, White Roof

Established c 1926, operating only between Kirkcaldy and Burntisland. Acquired by GMC on 15th December 1930.

Vehicles:

aq 3.26	SP9709	?	?	?	B14	ex Anderson Methil; Dst by fire 11.27
?	SP 646	Albion	?	?	?	ni
.26	XS1719	Gilford	?	?	B-F	to GMC (–) later (Y28) Sold 2.32
.26	XS1720	Gilford	?	?	B-F	to GMC (24) later (Y29)
?3.29	FG4753	Albion PKA26	5075L	?	B26F	to GMC (26)

146. *Harrow & Stocks' Gilford XS 1720, Kirkcaldy Esplanade, in the late twenties. The photo – although damaged – is the only record of this small company.*

HAY'S BUS SERVICE
John Hay, Lundin Links

Livery: Fawn

Established c 1928, operating Leven to Anstruther by Colinsburgh and Arncroach. Purchased by Harris of Leven c 1935.

Vehicles:

aq .28	?	Reo	?	?	B26F	ex Cormie
11.28	FG4484	Bean	1690/11W	?	B19F	ni
?	?	Gilford	?	?	?	ni
?	SN- - - -	Albion	?	?	?	ex McLellan Spittalfield

HOUSTON'S MOTOR SERVICE (HMS)
A Houston & Sons, Windygates

Livery: Blue lower panels, red mid band, white roof

Joe Houston drove for Finlay Brown then c 1923 with father and brothers formed A Houston & Sons to operate independently. Following death of A Houston the business (with then six vehicles) was sold to Finlay Brown.

Routes:

Windygates — Leven via Methilhill and Innerleven
Leven — Star of Markinch
Leven — Cupar via Montraive
Leven — St Andrews via Windygates, New Gliston and Peat Inn

Vehicles:

c .23	?	Ford	?	?	B14F	ni
?	?	Reo	?	?	B14F	ni
?	?	Fiat	?	?	?	ni
c .24	VA2973	Reo	?	?	B14F	to Brown
6.26	FG1774	Chevrolet	X8677	?	B14F	to Brown
10.26	FG2255	Reo	?	?	B20	to Brown
aq .26	SN3545	Albion PJ24	?	?	B24	ex Northern General, to Brown
aq .27	UI1928	Albion PM28	7018B	?	B32R	ex Londonderry cpm; to Brown
12.28	FG4585	Albion PKA26	5069I	?	B26F	to Brown

147. *The blue, red and white livery of Houston's Albion FG 4585 is well shown in this view in Windygates.*

148. *Kirkcaldy Esplanade terminus with Jack Brothers' Reo FG 5256, which was new in June 1928.*

JACK BROTHERS
David, Jas and Wm Jack, Mitchell Street, Kirkcaldy

Livery: Dark Blue

Commenced as a taxi business, then charabancs purchased for hire. Stage services started September 1928. Acquired the business of David Glendinning of Kinghorn. Jack Brothers bought by Alexander, November 1931.

Routes:

Kirkcaldy Town Service; Kirk Wynd — Macindoe Crescent
Kirkcaldy — Burntisland

Vehicles:

?	?	?	?	?	ch36	ni
6.28	FG4256	Reo	5964	?	B20F	ni
aq	?	W & G Du Cross	?	?	B14	ex Glendinning
aq	?	W & G Du Cross	?	?	B14	ex Glendinning

MILLER'S BUS SERVICE
Jas B Miller, St Clair Street, Kirkcaldy

Former Cousin's driver who possibly operated Kirkcaldy to Kinghorn for short period with 20-seat Ford bus. No further details known.

LEGGATES
Jim Leggate, Methil

Possibly operated Kirkcaldy to Leven for a short period with a Dennis bus. No further details known.

Livery: Bright Yellow

Established 1921 operating from Leven to Markinch. Successful operation led to expansion and eventually purchased by Alexander 1 April 1932, with GMC being used as the operating company.

Routes:
  Leven – Markinch (by 1921) extended to Leslie (by ?)
  Leven – Kinross (from 7.27) extended to Perth (from 5.28)
  Kirkcaldy – Leslie

Vehicles:

	c .21	?	Ford	?	?	ch	'The Milton Violet'
	.21	SP2174	Ford 'T'	?	?	B14	Sold 1.26
	?	?	Karrier	?	?	ch/lry	ex Saline MS
	5.24	SP8980	Lancia	?	?	B-F	To Alexander (O153)
	3.25	SP9951	Lancia	?	Metcalfe	B-F	Scr 12.31
	6.25	FG 524	Reo	?	?	B16F	ni
	.26	ES8191	Lancia	508	Crerar	B26F	to Alexander (O152)
	?	?	Lancia	?	Crerar	?	ni
	?	?	Lancia	?	Crerar	?	ni
10	5.26	FG1783	Thornycroft A1	12794	Grant, Cameron & Curle	B20F	to Alexander (O151)
11	5.27	FG2877	Thornycroft	13471	Grant, Cameron & Curle	B32F	to Alexander (O143)
13	5.28	FG3975	Thornycroft A6	16237	?	?	to Alexander (O150)
12	11.28	FG4476	Thornycroft BC	16307	Vickers	B32F	to Alexander (O144)
4	7.29	FG5281	Thornycroft A6	18206	Park Royal?	B24	to Alexander (O146)
14	10.29	FG5457	Thornycroft BC	18793	Park Royal?	B31R	to Alexander (O145)
15	11.29	FG5458	Leyland LT1	50678	Jackson	B30F	to Alexander (N132)
16	aq .30	VU 719	Crossley Alpha	90291	Crossley	?	to Alexander (O142)

149. *Dating from 1925 was this 16-seat Reo FG 524. David Eadie was proud of his buses and had photographs taken of many of them.*

150. *Lancia ES 8191 was purchased in 1926, licensed in Perth by Crerar of Crieff, who built the 26-seat body.*

151. *This rear view of FG 2877, a 1927 Thornycroft, shows, in small print, that it had Fife Licence 162 – also the badge with the silhouette of Markinch Parish Church.*

152. *Milton fleet No 12 was this 1928 Thornycroft FG 4476 32-seater with bodywork by Vickers. It became Alexander's O144 and lasted until 1936.*

MORRIS'S
G W S Morris, Broadleys, Crail

Crail to Balcomie Golf Course generally, with Saturdays only runs from Crail to St Andrews.

Vehicle:

?	?	Morris	?	?	ch14	ni	
?	FG8344	Morris	?	?	B?F	ni	

MURDOCH
Wm Murdoch, Wellesley Road, Methil

Established by summer of 1920 — potato merchant with charabanc body for lorry. Ran Buckhaven to Glenfarg — possibly on private hires only.

Vehicles:

?	SP1944	Albion	?	?	ch/lry	ni	
5.21	?	Albion	?	?	ch30	ni	

153. *Wm Murdoch's lorry / charabanc — the temporary nature of the charabanc body is obvious.*

154. *Ramage's 1927 Reo FG 3391 in St Andrews en route to Buckhaven — probably in 1931.*

RAMAGE'S BUS SERVICE
David Ramage, Largo Road, Lundin Links

Livery: Brown

Established by December 1924; not acquired by Alexander until February 1936.

Routes:
Leven — St Andrews via Largo and Largowood (from 12.24) to Kirkcaldy (from 2.28)
became Buckhaven to St Andrews (from 10.30)

Vehicles:

c .24	?	Bean	?	?	B14	ni
6.27	FG3391	Reo	146450	?	B14F	ni
aq 10.29	FG5459	Chevrolet	59079	?	B14F	ex Alexander
12.30	FG6515	Leyland TA4	66740	?	B20	to Alexander (O268)
12.32	FG8135	Dennis Lancet	170223	Alex Mtrs	B32R	to Alexander (O267)
6.34	FG9576	Leyland LT5A	4203	Alexander	B32R	to Alexander (N166)
6.35	AFG894	Dennis Ace	200403	Dennis	C20	to Alexander (O269)

RAMSAY'S
Jas Ramsay, Leslie

Operated Kirkcaldy — Leslie, from (probably) 1923 until acquired by Simpsons MS c. January 1928.

Vehicle:

4.23	SP7749	?	?	?	to Simpsons 1.28

RONALDSON
E R Ronaldson, Central Garage, Kirkcaldy

Established as operator c. May 1922 — local coachbuilder whose attempt to operate a stage service did not survive long. No bus bodies were built by Ronaldson so far as is known.

Routes:
Kirkcaldy to Auchtertool (by May 1922)
then Kirkcaldy to Kinglassie (by October 1923)

Vehicle:

c .22	?	?	?	?	ch14	ni

Established July 1913 operating between Leven and East Wemyss from 2 October 1913, in opposition to the Wemyss Tramways. As fares were higher, service less frequent, and roads unmade, the enterprise was not successful. It was some years ahead of its time. The first run was marred by '. . . a piece of carelessness saw water instead of petrol being put into the tank . . . much good time was wasted as the carburettor had to be taken down . . .' An inauspicious start.

Regular stage operation did not continue for long and the one vehicle was then utilised on tour and private hire work. No further details known.

Vehicle:

| c 7.13 | ? | ? | ? | ? | ch30 | ni |

155. *Members of the Smith family with four of their early Reos, from the left SP 9878, FG 413, SP 9496, GD 255 – in a variety of liveries. Photographed at the entrance to Ravenscraig Park, Kirkcaldy.*

156. *Reo No 3, SP 9496, 'The Silver Queen' showing the silver livery with maroon mid band. Richard (Dick) Smith in charge.*

SMITH'S MOTORWAYS (also KIRKCALDY MOTOR BUS SERVICE)   W&J R Smith, Ravenscraig Street, Kirkcaldy

Livery: Initially Silver Grey with Maroon Band, then Brown and Orange later the Brown became 'Mid-Blue'.

J R Smith had been a driver with ABC Co and Andersons prior to commencing on his own account as a 'chaser' on the Wemmys tram route during 1923. Brothers Tom, Richard (Dick) and Harry were also heavily involved in the business. At one stage operated also from Montrose to Forfar but sold this part of the undertaking to Cormie Bros. Smith's were one of the first operators to challenge Kirkcaldy Corporation by starting — without permission — a Town Service from 21 December 1927. A Glasgow service was planned but the idea abandoned when Cormie commenced operating that route. Business acquired by Alexander 1 June 1931, operation vested in GMC.

Routes:
    Kirkcaldy (Gallatown) — Leven (by 12.23)
    Kirkcaldy to Leslie via Markinch (from 6.26)
    Kirkcaldy to Auchtermuchty via Falkirk (from 5.27) extended to Perth (7.27)
    Kirkcaldy Town Service (Kirk Wynd to Gallagown)

Vehicles:

1	.23	?	Ford 'T'	?	?	B14F	ni
2	.24	GD 255	Reo	?	?	B14F	ex Demonstrator
3	9.24	SP9496	Reo	?	Eaton	B14F	'The Silver Queen'
4	.25	VA2973	Reo	?	?	B14F	'The Silver King'
5	3.25	SP9878	Reo	112321	Eaton	B14F	ni
6	5.26	FG 413	Reo	?	?	?	ni
?	?	GD8848	Fiat	?	?	?	ni
?	?	?	Chevrolet	?	?	?	ni
?	?	?	Chevrolet	?	?	?	ni
?	?	?	Gilford	?	?	?	ni
?	?	?	Lancia	?	Crerar ?	?	ni
?	?	?	Lancia	?	Crerar ?	?	ni
?	?	?	Lancia	?	Crerar ?	?	ni
?	?	?	De Dion	?	?	?	? ni
?	2.27	FG2585	W & G DuCross	L2566	?	B26F	Scr 9.31
?	2.27	?	W & G DuCross	?	?	?	ni
18	5.27	FG3095	Studebaker	317400S	?	B20F	to Alexander (O199)
?	7.28	FG4288	Reo FAX	5863	?	B20	ni
19	8.28	FG4402	Talbot	2620	?	B26F	ni
19	11.28	FG4535	Leyland PLC1	47570	Kelly	B25F	Exhibited at 1928 Motor Show; to WA (M9)
21	4.29	FG4921	Crossley Eagle	90020	Cadogan	B32	to Alexander (O175)
?	4.29	FG4935	Crossley Eagle	90019	Dickson	B32F	to Alexander (O174)
28	7.29	FG5308	Crossley Eagle	90035	Horsfield	B-F	to Alexander (O172)
26	12.29	FG5616	Daimler CF6	7152S	Hall Lewis	B32R	to Alexander (O146)
25	1.30	FG5665	Daimler CF6	7150S	Hall Lewis	B32R	to Alexander (O151)
27	2.30	FG5730	Daimler CF6	7122S	Hall Lewis	B32R	To Alexander (O145) ex demonstrator TY6406
30	3.30	FG5787	Crossley Eagle	90054	Crossley	B32	to Alexander (O171)
18	5.30	FG6110	Daimler CF6	7120S	Hall Lewis	B32	to Alexander (O150) ex demonstrator TY6403
31	12.30	FG6511	Crossley Alpha	90292	Cadogan	B32	to Alexander (O164)
32	1.31	FG6596	Crossley Alpha	90601	Cadogan	B32	to Alexander (O163)

(A Karrier was operated — for 3 days — then returned.)

157. *Smith operated this smart Talbot (FG 4402) which was numbered 19 for a time; the fleet contained similar vehicles but made by 'W & G Du Cross'. Behind follows a Wemyss Tramways Albion.*

158. *Magnificent Leyland FG 4535 – which was exhibited at the 1928 Motor Show. Seen here in Tay Street, Perth on the service to Kirkcaldy. (also numbered 19!)*

159. *Crossley Eagle FG 5308 of 1929 became number 28 in the large Smiths' fleet. Also photographed in Perth. Driver W Webster.*

160. *Two of Smith's buses on Kirkcaldy Esplanade. In front is No 27, Daimler FG 5730, which carried Smith's name only from February 1930 until June 1931.*

STEPHEN'S

J B Stephen, Dysart

Probable operator, Gallatown to Leven commenced November 1923. No further information.

STEWART'S MOTORS

John W Stewart, 17 Rose Street, Kirkcaldy

Livery: Dark Blue

Acquired business of Harrow Scott in July 1925 (with one bus); sold to A & R Forrester in April 1927 (with then two buses).

Routes:
    Dunfermline to Burntisland (former Harrow Scott route)
    Kirkcaldy to Kinross via Lochore
    Kirkcaldy to Kinglassie via Cluny

Vehicles:

aq 7.25	SP9283	Reo	?	?	B14F	ex Harrow Scott
?	?	Albion	?	?	?	ni
?	GM 704	Karrier	?	?	B20	to Forrester 4.27
?	?	Lancia	?	Stewart ?	?	ni

161. *Lancia belonging to Stewart's Motors of Kirkcaldy passing through Cardenden, being chased by one of GMC's Caledons. The business existed from July 1925 to April 1927 only.*

SYME'S

William Syme, Kirkcaldy

Possibly workers route Kirkcaldy to Kinglassie. Wm Syme later was driver with Forrester's, then Simpson's & Forrester's, then Alexander. No further details known.

TOD'S

J M Tod, Seafield Tower Works, Kirkcaldy

Established 1913, operating tours, but advertised a service from Kirkcaldy to Markinch (commencing 7 November 1914). This may have operated until 1916 at least. Date of cessation not known.

Vehicles:

?	SP 354	Albion	?	Hunter	ch28	ni
?	SP4369	Albion	?	?	ch32	body to Harris, Leven

162. *This was the first of Tod's Albions, with which he started a service from Kirkcaldy to Markinch in November 1914. The fashions appear to date this scene as somewhat later.*

Livery: (buses) Dark Red and Cream

After the First World War rampant bus 'poaching' or chasing on the highly-trafficced tram route led to considerable loss of passenger income. To combat this a fleet of Tilling-Stevens buses was put on the road with a view to 'seeing-off' the opposition. These tended to be slower than the opposition and smaller, faster vehicles were obtained.

A policy of acquisition of the small independent competitors was actively pursued, commencing with Caley Motor Co in April 1925. The controlling interest in the largest local bus undertaking – GMC of Kirkcaldy – was achieved in February 1926, but this Company (and A & R Motors acquired May 1927) continued to operate independently but with more co-ordinated operation.

Balfour Beatty who maintained the controlling interest in the Fife Tramway Light and Power Company (of which Wemyss Tramways was a subsidiary) in April 1931 passed control of all their Fife bus subsidiaries to Alexander. Assets and vehicles were lodged with GMC, the local 'operations' Company. The Wemyss Company was wound up in July 1938.

Routes:

Kirkcaldy (Gallatown) – Leven (8.22) – Largo (9.23) – Anstruther (7.24)
Kirkcaldy (Gallatown) – Auchtermuchty via Falkland (from 4.27)
Kirkcaldy Terminus moved to Sands Road (Esplanade) from 29.10.23
Buckhaven – St Andrews via Largo (from 7.28)
Anstruther – Glasgow via Kirkcaldy, and Stirling (from 6.29) joint with SGO Co
Leven – Auchtermuchty, becomes Buckhaven – Perth via Auchtermuchty (6.29)
Leven – Leslie via Markinch

Vehicles: *These vehicles to GMC 6.32

No.	Date	Reg	Make/Model	Chassis	Body	Seating	Notes
	7.22	SP7216	Tilling-Stevens	?	Strachan & Brown	B29F	Scr 10.28
	7.22	SP7217	Tilling-Stevens	?	Strachan & Brown	B29F	Scr 10.28
3	7.22	SP7218	Tilling-Stevens	?	Strachan & Brown	B29F	Sold 9.30
	6.23	SP8084	Tilling-Stevens TS5	?	Strachan & Brown	B29F	Sold 10.30
	6.23	SP8085	Tilling-Stevens	?	Strachan & Brown	B29F	Sold 4.30
	6.23	SP8086	Tilling-Stevens TS5	2831	Strachan & Brown	B29F	Sold (?)
	6.24	SP9168	Tilling-Stevens	?	Strachan & Brown	Ch25	Sold 5.31
	7.24	SP9217	Tilling-Stevens	2250	Strachan & Brown	Ch25	Sold
	7.24	SP9218	Tilling-Stevens	?	Strachan & Brown	Ch25	Sold 11.30
	7.24	SP9262	Tilling-Stevens	?	?	B29F	Sold 7.31
	7.24	SP9278	Tilling-Stevens TS3A	3217	?	?	ni Scr 9.50
	7.24	SP9279	Tilling-Stevens	?	?	?	Sold 8.30
	4.25	FG 123	Halley QSX	2963	?	B20F	ni
	4.25	FG 124	Halley QSX	2965	?	B20F	ni
	5.25	FG 125	Halley QSX	2967	?	B20F	*
14	5.25	FG 126	Halley QSX	2968	?	B20F	ni
	1.26	FG1157	Albion ?	?	?	?	Scr 3.28
15	6.26	FG1909	Albion PJ26	5012D	?	Ch19	*; (C191); (D107) wd .33
16	6.26	FG1937	Albion PJ26	5010A	?	B25F	*; (C189); (D66) wd .32
17	6.26	FG1938	Albion PJ26	5012A	?	B25F	*; (C197); (D70) wd .32
	aq 4.26	SP8343	Daimler ?	?	?	?	ex Caley M Co Sold 11.26 ?psv
	aq 11.26	SP4886	Tilling-Stevens ?	?	?	?	ex Caley M Co Scr 10.28
	aq 1.27	SP4592	?	?	?	?	ex Rolland Sold 7.32 ?psv
18	7.26	FG1939	Albion PJ26	5013A	Cowieson?	B25F	*; (C196); (F70) wd .33
19	7.26	FG1940	Albion PJ26	5013B	?	B25F	*; (C192); wd .33
	5.28	FG4063	Halley JO	3066	?	B20F	*;
	5.28	FG4064	Halley JO	3068	?	B20F	*; (0212); wd .32
23	5.28	FG4116	Halley QSX	3002	?	B20F	*; (0213); wd .32
21	5.28	FG4117	Albion PJ26	5065B	?	B25F	*; (C118); wd .36
22	5.28	FG4118	Albion PJ26	5065C	?	B25F	*; (C190); wd .37
	aq 6.29	SP2877	Halley	?	?	B32	*; ex SGO Co, ex Cousins
	aq 6.29	SP4901	Halley	?	?	Ch?	*; ex SGO Co, ex Cousins
	aq 6.29	FG 243	Minerva	?	?	B20	ex SGO Co, ex Cousins Scr 9.31
	aq 1.30	SP6106	Daimler ?	?	?	?	ex Caley M Co; Sold 7.32
	aq .31	FG4113	Albion PJ26	5064G	?	B29F	*; ex Peattie Bros; Sold 7.32

163. *Wemyss Tilling-Stevens bus SP 7218 photographed when brand-new, in front of the tram depot at Aberhill.*

164. *One of the Wemyss Company's four Halleys, FG 125 also photographed in the yard at Aberhill.*

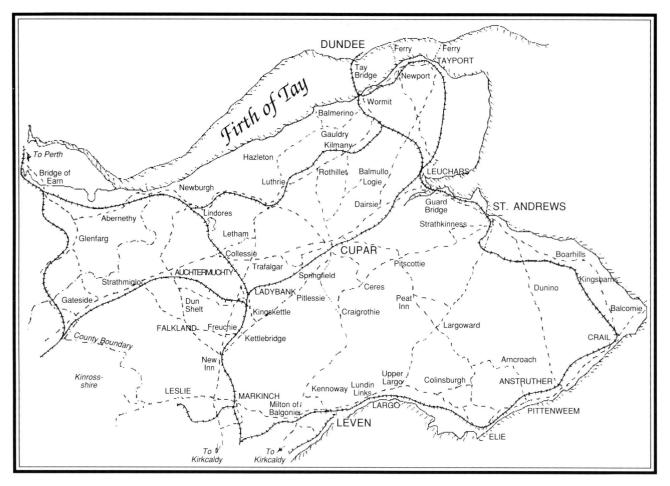

165. *Map of Bus Routes in North Fife.*

Timetables for the Cupar area, February 1928.

BUS OPERATORS - NORTH FIFE

BAYNE
Robert Bayne, Tayport

Operated Tayport and Newport Pier (for Dundee Ferry)
No further details.
Only vehicle recorded 'T' Ford with 12-seat body.

CENTRAL GARAGE
William C Smith, Crossgate, Cupar

Livery: Maroon and White

Garage business which purchased its first charabone in July 1920 for touring work. First stage service operated from September 1923. May have acquired business of Sharps Motors of Cupar (q.v.) in April 1929. Business purchased by SMT in June 1930, thereafter operated under Simpson's and Forrester's organisation, retaining W C Smith as local manager.

Routes:

Cupar – Kettlebridge via Ladybank (9.23) – Falkland (11.26)
Cupar – Falkland via Pitlessie (5.25)
Cupar – Lundin Links (5.25) Summer Saturdays only
Cupar – Balmullo (.26) – Newport (3.27)
Cupar – Letham via Springfield and Trafalgar (.26) – Ladybank (5.28)
Cupar – Newport via Guardbridge and Leuchars (7.26)
becomes Kirkcaldy – Newport via Markinch, Cupar, Guardbridge and Leuchars (12.29)
Cupar – Elie via Largoward (4.30) – former Sharp route

Vehicles:

7.20	?	?	?	?	ch/lry	ni
.23	?	?	?	?	ch	ni
6.23	SP7989	Karrier	?	?	ch	ni
11.26	FG2301	Karrier	CL35012	?	B26F	to S & F (60)
7.28	FG4300	Minerva	?	?	B25	to S & F (59)
7.29	FG5333	Minerva	28030	?	B30	to S & F (58)
10.29	FG5459	Chevrolet	59079	?	Ch14	eventually to W Alexander
10.29	FG5468	Chevrolet	59093	?	Ch14	to Davidson, Kirkcaldy
1.30	FG5678	Mercedez Benz	1125/13	?	B	to S & F (61)
?	VA6967	Minerva	?	?	?	to S & F (62)

166. *Few Karriers operated in Fife but FG 2301 of Central Garage, Cupar was snapped in the town waiting to set off on the run to Falkland.*

167. *Not the best photo, but a record of Clow's Bedford FG 7975, after becoming W 31 in Alexander's fleet.*

CLOW'S MOTORS
John M Clow, Edenside, Guardbridge

Livery: Grey

Established 1922, operating between St Andrews and Newport (Ferry) via Guard Bridge and Leuchars (shared latterly with GMC and arranged to meet alternate ferries). Acquired by Alexander April 1935.

Vehicles:

?	?	Gilford	?	?	B18	ni
?	?	Gilford	?	?	B20	ni
6.27	ES9628	Lancia	?	Crerar	B26	ni
?	?	Laffley	?	?	?	ni
?	?	Cottin et Desgouttes	?	Crerar ?	B30?	ni
?	TS6528	Albion	?	?	C20F	ex Dickson, Dundee
7.32	FG7975	Bedford	?	Economy	B25	to Alexander (W31)

168. *The first bus owned by Stanley Fuller was this neat 14-seat Ford, seen here in Falkland in September 1922.*

169. *In May 1923 this 14-seat Ford Model 'T' charabanc was purchased, registered SP 7947.*

170. *A most unusual vehicle – possibly unique in Fife was Fuller's 'United' charabanc, an American chassis probably registered by Crerar of Crieff who built the bodywork.*

171. *This smart Commer FG 3660 was Fuller's last purchase, in February 1928. It served after May of that year with GMC, who acquired Fuller's business then.*

COLLIE'S
George A Collie, Wormit

Long established horse brake proprietor and posting establishment. Possibly sold to Robertson.

Routes:
- Wormit – Hazleton via Gauldry (by 1931)
- Wormit – Balmerino (by 1931) to connect with morning and evening train
- Balmerino – Newport (for Ferry) (by 1931)

Vehicles:

?	?	Lancia	?	?	ch	ni
?	?	Albion	?	Kemp & Nicholson	B20	Sold to Robertson

DELAMERE
Delamere, Leuchars

Stated to have operated Leuchars -- St Andrews. No other information known.

FULLER'S MOTORS
Stanley Fuller, Newburgh

Livery: Dark Red

Taxi operator who commenced a bus run to Perth. Purchased by GMC Kirkcaldy in July 1928 (*prior* to any Alexander acquisitions) and operated independently for some time thereafter although GMC vehicles were brought to the Newburgh garage.

Routes:
- Newburgh – Perth (from c. 22) (became St Andrews – Newburgh – Perth via Strathmiglo (Jan. 3.27)
- Newburgh – Markinch via Falkland

Vehicles:

.22	?	Ford 'T'	?	?	B14F	ni
5.23	SP7947	Ford 'T'	?	?	ch14	ni
?	?	Cottin et Desgouttes	?	Crerar?	?	ni
.24	ES6853	United	?	Crerar?	ch	ni
?	XX3822	De Dion	?	?	ch	ni
4.26	FG1652	Dodge	D111594	Strachan & Brown	B20	to GMC
5.26	FG1765	Berliet	29052	Crerar?	B20	to GMC
12.26	FG2389	Chevrolet	?	?	?	to GMC
3.27	FG2588	Dodge	A754854	Park Royal	B20	ni
3.27	FG2589	Dodge	A754067	Park Royal	B20	ni
?	?	AEC	?	?	?	ni
2.28	FG3660	Commer	?	?	B-F	to GMC

GLENDINNING

Verbal report of operation between Cupar and Anstruther via Dunino. No further details.

GRANT'S BUS SERVICE
C M Grant & Sons (later A Grant), Cupar Arms Garage, Burnside, Cupar

Livery: Navy Blue

Horse brakes operated from stables at Cupar Arms Hotel, garage from c 1914. Purchased first charabanc in 1920 and commenced regular service from Cupar to St Andrews, Thursdays and Saturdays only from May to November 1921 (1s 6d single). Became weekly service from May 1922, subsequently daily. Acquired by Alexander May 1930, operations vested in Simpson's & Forrester's.

Routes:
- Cupar – St Andrews via Dairsie and Guardbridge (5.21)
- Cupar – Newport (6.23)
- Cupar – Springfield (11.24) Saturdays only
- Cupar – Luthrie via Rathillet (9.26) Saturdays only
- Cupar – Logie (11.26) Saturdays only
- Cupar – Ladybank (7.28)

Vehicles:

3.20	?	?	?	?	ch14	ni
11.20	?	?	?	?	B20	ni
11.22	?	?	?	?	ch32	ni
?	?	Fiat	?	?	B14	Dstd by fire 1.30
?	?	Fiat	?	?	?	ni
4.25	FG 166	Lancia	?	Crerar	B32	ni
?	?	Lancia	?	Crerar	B32	ni
?	?	Reo	?	?	?	ni
?	?	Crossley	?	?	B26?	ni

172 . *Johnstone's Vulcan bus FG 3689. The funnel of the Tay Ferry can be seen over the sea wall at Newport.*

173 . *Twelve-seat charabanc owned by Peter Robertson of Gauldry, on a trip to the Bien Inn, Glenfarg.*

JOHNSTONE'S David Y Johnstone, Tay Street, Tayport

Established before 1927, operating initially to and from Newport Ferry. Acquired by Alexander April 1935.

Routes:
    Newport – Tayport
    Newport – Wormit (some runs Wormit – Tayport)
    Newport – St Andrews (by 12.30)

Vehicles:

?	?	Ford 'T'	?	?	B12R	ni	
3.28	FG3689	Vulcan	3XB/82	?	B20F	ex Clark, Glencraig	
?	?	Albion	?	?	?	ni	

ROBERTSON'S Peter Robertson, Main Street, Gauldry

Commenced with taxis then had charabanc built onto Ford 'T' chassis. Obtained contract for schools work then commenced a link to Wormit, meeting morning, lunchtime and evening trains. May have taken over Collies operation. Business to Williamson (still in business, now trading as Moffat and Williamson) c 1946.

Routes:
    Gauldry – Wormit Station
    Gauldry – Newport (for Ferry) Saturdays and Sundays only

Vehicles:

?	?	Ford 'T'	?	Lamb	?	ni
?	?	Chevrolet	?	Alexander?	B14	ni
.33	YJ 539	Bedford	?	?	B20	ni
?	?	Bedford	?	?	?	ex Birrell, Markinch
?	?	Albion	?	Kemp & Nicholson	B20	ex Collie, Wormit

SHARP'S MOTORS Wm H Sharp, 26 Crossgate, Cupar

Established c 1924 operating initially to and from Stratheden Hospital. Ladybank route subjected to competition from Grants. Operation of Elie route taken up by Central Garage Co which may signify a take over of some description.

Routes:
    Cupar – Springfield via Stratheden (c 1924)
    Cupar – Ladybank (21.7.28) – Kingskettle (5.29)
    Cupar – Elie via Peat Inn, Largowood, Colinsburgh (3.29)

Vehicles:

1.24	SP8956	?	?	?	B14	to Bankfoot Motor Co 7.28
?	?	?	?	?	B14	Dstd by fire 12.28
4.26	FG1429	De Dion	410	?	B20	ni
aq 2.29	?	De Dion	?	?	B20	ex Dickson, Dundee; returned 3.29

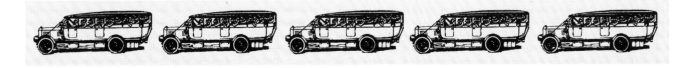

OPERATORS BASED OUTWITH FIFE

1. HARPER OF TILLICOULTRY — Tillicoultry to Dunfermline
2. CRERAR OF CRIEFF — Crieff to St Andrews
3. PETERS OF MILNATHORT — Milnathort to Cupar
4. STAR MS OF GLASGOW — Stirling (later Glasgow) to St Andrews
5. SCOTTISH GENERAL OMNIBUS CO OF LARBERT — Glasgow to Lochore, Glasgow to Anstruther etc.
6. W ALEXANDER & SONS OF FALKIRK — Glasgow to Lochore

174. *A fine example of Jackson's bodywork is seen on FG 6950 licensed in May 1931 to D Harper of Tillicoultry, who operated into Dunfermline. A Morris Viceroy, it was photographed outside the agents, Fife Motor Company in Halbeath Road before entering service.*

175. *Interior of Jackson's works in Mill Street, Dunfermline, Fife's foremost bus bodybuilders. In the foreground is Vulcan FG 3689, formerly with D Clark of Glencraig, which appears to be being gone over prior to sale to Johnstone of Tayport. In the door at left rear is a vehicle belonging to Pioneer Services of Thurso, founded by T W Knox from Torryburn.*

OPERATORS OPERATING TOURS ONLY

1. HAMILTON OF ST ANDREWS
2. GREIG OF ELIE
3. CUTHBERT OF ANSTRUTHER
4. LEGGATE BROS OF METHIL
5. DESCAMPS OF KIRKCALDY
6. LINDSAY OF KIRKCALDY
7. MILLER OF KIRKCALDY
8. SIMPSONS OF KIRKCALDY
9. WHITELAW OF KIRKCALDY
10. SCOTT OF KIRKCALDY
11. WESTWATER OF DYSART
12. R & D COACHES OF ROSYTH
13. McKERCHER OF FREUCHIE

Other tour operators probably existed.

176. *Typical of touring operators' vehicles was Johnny Westwater's Reo SP 9968, seen in Dysart with a fashionably-dressed party.*

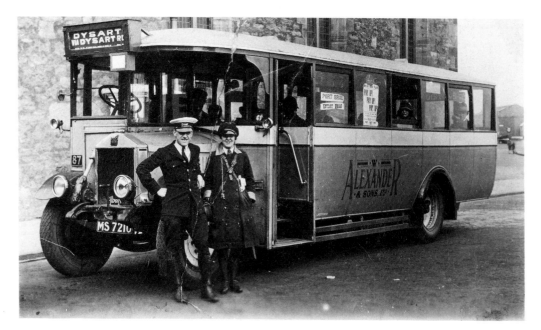

177. *May 1931, replacing the Kirkcaldy trams on the Dysart route was Alexander's Albion MS 7210 (No 87), formerly owned by the Scottish General Omnibus Co., with Driver Davidson, at Port Brae. The advert on the side window demands 'Pay up' for Kirkcaldy's annual Hospital Pageant.*

SOURCE MATERIAL

In and Out of Fifeshire by Charabanc		G Eyre-Todd
The Roads of Fife	Owen Silver	J Donald 1987
The Railways of Fife	Wm S Brown	Melven Press 1980
Fife Looks Ahead	Fife C C 1946	
Dunfermline Magistrates' Minutes		
Fife Free Press		
Fife News		
West Fife News		
Fife Herald		
Dunfermline Press		
Dunfermline Register		
West Fife Echo		
Leven Advertiser & Wemyss Gazette		
Commercial Motor		
Motor Traction		
Motor Transport Year Book & Directory		

ASSISTANCE

Harry Adamson	David Eadie	D McGregor
Ian Armstrong	R S Fowler	J Malcolm
R Atkinson	A Elder	R Maule
J M Barclay	J Fotheringham	Mrs E May
Robert Bernard	R Forrester	Mrs Miller
Mrs Beveridge	Martin Gardner	Bob Miller
Miss Bissett	J Gillespie	J Philp
Mrs W A Brotchie	R L Grieves	Dr R A Read
J K D Blair	W B Grubb	A Roper
Bill Brown	R M Henderson	Bob Scott
James Brown	D L G Hunter	J R Smith
R Brown	David Johnstone	Bert Syme
W Cormie	J Kilgour	Mrs Turpie
John Cousins	Jim King	Dave West
Mat Cousins	Wm King	G Wallace
Findlay Coutts	Jim Lamb	Mrs Williamson
Jas T Dawson	R M Livingston	Alex Young

PHOTO CREDITS

Permission to reproduce photographs is recorded with thanks to:

R L Grieves Collection, 3, 6, 31, 43, 76, 77, 78, 79, 80, 81, 82, 84, 87, 90, 91, 92, 93, 98, 99, 102, 104, 105, 108, 120, 121, 122, 127, 128, 129, 135, 141, 152, 155, 156, 158: J Blyth, 8, 161: G Waugh Collection, 10, 36, 95: Kirkcaldy Libraries Collection, 17: Mrs J Sneddon, 30: W B Grubb Collection, 32: Dunfermline Libraries Collection, 42: Mrs Niven, 46: Kirkcaldy Museums Collection, 53: Aberdeen Transport Society Collection, 111, 167: Mr M Gardner, 123, 124, 125: M Morton Hunter Collection, 137: Mr D Johnstone, 172. All other from NB Traction Group Collection.

Tickets on page 33 mostly from the collection of Roger Atkinson.

Illustration on rear cover reproduced by kind permission of the Dunfermline Press.

General Motor Carrying Co.
Limited.

MOTOR 'BUS PROPRIETORS.

DIRECTORS.
W.J.Thomson,J.P.   W.Alexander.
J.H.Followe,C.B.E.,M.V.O.   W.Alexander,Jr.
J.Calder.   J.C.Sword.   J A.Lindsay,D.L.,J.P.

TELEPHONE NOS:-
Kirkcaldy 2095, 2096, Newburgh 21,
Leven 58, 180, Markinch 43,
Anstruther 55, Kelty 15.

Milton of Balgonie,

Markinch,   19

Closing of Depôt.

All persons employed here, other than those already selected, are warned that their services will terminate any day from now on.

The last act — removed from the notice board, after closure of Eadie's garage.